Frances Clark Center
for Keyboard Pedagogy

Thank you for your support of the
first printing of *The Success Factor*
by Elvina T. Pearce.

WHAT EXPERTS ARE SAYING ABOUT *THE SUCCESS FACTOR IN PIANO TEACHING: MAKING PRACTICE PERFECT*

When parents settle for an inexperienced teacher until there's evidence their child is talented, Elvina Pearce lets them know they should instead find the "best educated, most experienced and most talented <u>teacher</u> they can find." Reading this book is like having extraordinary one-on-one conversations with perhaps the most talented teacher of our era. Her knowledge and experience are evident on every page and her common sense ideas about "self-directed" practice, "thinking tempo," "purposeful repetition," and "impulse practice" are just a few of her countless "gems" to make teachers feel they are in the same room with her during every chapter of this book. Just as Richard Chronister and Frances Clark shared their expertise with us, Elvina Pearce continues this tradition and conveys the best practices of talented teachers. This book is a gift to all of us who aspire to be a talented teacher.

Brenda Dillon, Project Director, National Piano Foundation
Author and clinician in group teaching and Recreational Music Making

* * *

Whether a novice teacher, or one who has had years of experience, everyone can benefit from the sound advice offered by the highly respected author of The Success Factor in Piano Teaching: Making Practice Perfect. *Elvina Truman Pearce offers readers a comprehensive pedagogy course in a book! From her knowledgeable perspective as a teacher who has had outstanding training and extensive experience as a collegiate teacher, independent teacher and performer, she is able to provide readers priceless information and philosophies that can elevate their teaching. Ideas are vividly brought to life through her descriptive scenarios and musical examples. She also generously shares many of the strategies and studio documents that have been so beneficial to her teaching. The book promotes approaches that will help students become independent and proactive learners.* The Success Factor in Piano Teaching *is an essential resource and a significant addition to the pedagogical literature that belongs in every teacher's personal library and on the shelves of every music school library.*

Gail Berenson, NCTM, Ohio University
Past President, Music Teachers National Association

* * *

The first time I went to a workshop by Elvina Truman Pearce it was an absolute epiphany, and changed forever how I teach. I'm delighted that this book encapsulates her highly successful teaching approach for current and future piano teachers. Although not presented as a pedagogy textbook, it is a <u>must-read</u> for all piano teachers, no matter how long they have been teaching! Elvina's practical advice, teaching scenarios, and musical examples reveal her extensive experience and deep understanding of what it takes to be a successful piano teacher. Elvina generously shares the teaching approaches and philosophies that have made her one of the finest piano pedagogues of our time.

Rebecca Grooms Johnson, NCTM, President-Elect, Music Teachers National Association
Associate Editor, *Clavier Companion*

* * *

This text is a must for all piano pedagogy programs. It efficiently teaches the rudiments of how to teach beginner and intermediate level students. Using well-known literature, she analyzes pieces in a step by step manner to demonstrate what should be taught from week to week. Elvina has guided so many teachers over the course of her career. Her influence continues to resonate throughout the pedagogical world.

Helen Marlais, Grand Valley State University
Author-editor, *Succeeding with the Masters*

The Success Factor in Piano Teaching:

Making Practice Perfect

Photography by Raeleen H. Horn

Elvina Pearce
August 2014

The Success Factor in Piano Teaching:
Making Practice Perfect

By Elvina Truman Pearce

Foreword by Marvin Blickenstaff
Edited by Craig Sale

The Frances Clark Center for Keyboard Pedagogy, Inc.

Kingston, New Jersey

The Success Factor in Piano Teaching:
Making Practice Perfect

By Elvina Truman Pearce

Foreword by Marvin Blickenstaff

Edited by Craig Sale

Copyright ©2014

Published in the USA by
The Frances Clark Center for Keyboard Pedagogy, Inc.
P.O. Box 651
Kingston, New Jersey
Ph: 609.921.2900
Web: www.keyboardpedagogy.org

ISBN-13: 978-0615950761 (Custom Universal)
ISBN-10: 0615950760

Printed in the United States of America

Book design and cover design by Trevor Roberson, Trailhead Studio — THStudioDesign.com
Music typesetting by Alvin Trottman using Sibelius™
Photos of Ms. Pearce by Raeleen H. Horn

The Success Factor in Piano Teaching:

Making Practice Perfect

▲ CONTENTS

PART ONE: PEDAGOGY

What do successful teachers know?

Lesson Planning
Long range planning
The weekly lesson plan

Guidelines for parents of beginning piano students

Making adjustments
Characteristics of a typical transfer student
A transfer student's first lesson with the new teacher
Remedial work

"Time spent" *vs.* "Mind spent"
"Rules of the road" for productive self-directed practice

Fantasie in D Minor, K. 397 (Mozart)
The initial presentation at the lesson
Suggestions for practice and performance

Fantasy Dance, Op. 124, No. 5 (Schumann)
The initial presentation at the lesson
Suggestions for practice and performance

Notturno, Op. 54, No. 4 (Grieg)
The initial presentation at the lesson
Suggestions for practice and performance

Part I: Preparing to perform in studio recitals
   Choosing the music
   Maintenance practice
   Maintenance practice to retain secure memorization
   Recital decorum

Part II: Preparing to perform in competitions and auditions
   Some additional thoughts about the 21st century contest scenario

PART TWO: PROFESSIONALISM

What is the first step?
Where shall I teach?
Acquiring students: How do I get them?
How do I determine the amount of lesson fees?
Payment of fees

▲ CONTENTS

PART THREE: FINALE

▲ FOREWORD

The publication of *The Success Factor in Piano Teaching: Making Practice Perfect* is a heralded event in the field of piano pedagogy. Elvina Truman Pearce's experience as a performer, university professor, lecturer, composer, author, and teacher of students of all levels eminently qualifies her to write about successful teaching.

We often wish we could sit at the feet of great teachers, observing the process that renders their outstanding results. Most especially we wish to know how that process takes place with average students, a topic to which we relate most readily. Workshops and conference demonstrations are helpful, but these observations lack the day-to-day process of repertoire introduction to final performance, from demonstration of hand position to fluent scale and arpeggio playing.

Now, with the publication of this book, we can do exactly that. In these carefully crafted chapters, Elvina Pearce addresses virtually all aspects of our teaching and shows us the process that leads to success. With its emphasis on practice procedures, the title of the book is precise — *The Success Factor in Piano Teaching: Making Practice Perfect.* When our students engage in careful, thoughtful practice, successful music-making is the result. Teamwork is the clue: the teacher is the coach who understands the game inside and out. The students are the team, following the coach's game plan. In the end, we all win the trophy.

Elvina Pearce has lectured across the country and abroad. In the USA she has been a favorite clinician of piano teachers at national and regional conferences. When Richard Chronister, the co-founder of the National Conference on Piano Pedagogy, wished to program outstanding teaching demonstrations at the NCPP, he would call upon Elvina Pearce. In those sessions, her students performed beautifully, and her teaching showed us the careful way in which she introduces pieces, outlines effective practice steps, and progresses to finished, musical performances.

From the inaugural issue of *Keyboard Companion* in 1990, Elvina Pearce was an Associate Editor. When Richard Chronister died in 1999, she stepped forward and became the Editor-in-Chief, directing the successful publication of that journal for six years. Her articles have appeared in literally every American piano journal of the past forty years. Now much of the information which she presented in articles and workshops and teaching demonstrations is in this book for us to read, ponder, and put into practice with our own students.

It is the rare teacher who has studied with the most prominent artist teachers and also the pre-eminent teachers of piano pedagogy. Elvina Pearce brings that unusual combination to her students. As a young artist, she studied with the renowned Isabelle Vengerova. A summer pedagogy session by Frances Clark led to a lifelong collaboration with that great pedagogue. A rich combination, to say the least. One hears that legacy of artistry/pedagogy when her students perform and she shares this legacy with us in this book.

A perusal of the contents reveals the wide range of subjects addressed in *The Success Factor in Piano Teaching.* This is a no-stone-left-unturned pedagogical resource. The book also includes studio documents which Elvina Pearce sends to parents and to her students prior to performance, plus a meaningful year-end assessment which she writes for her own evaluation.

It is our privilege, as we read through the pages of *The Success Factor in Piano Teaching,* to sit at the feet of this remarkable teacher, and learn more about the process of success. It is our mandate to integrate these ideas into our own teaching for the betterment of our students.

—Marvin Blickenstaff

▲ EDITOR'S NOTE

When I reflect upon those teachers who had the greatest impact on my life, I see that they possessed not only great knowledge and expertise but also very distinct, captivating personalities. Included among these great teachers are Frances Clark, Louise Goss, and the author of *The Success Factor in Piano Teaching*, Elvina Truman Pearce. Although Elvina was never an official teacher of mine, she was my employer during my first years in the teaching profession and influenced my work in immeasurable ways.

It was with great honor that I accepted the task of preparing *The Success Factor in Piano Teaching* for publication. Never intended as a textbook, this book is similar to a series of workshops delivered in a conversational manner. As Marvin Blickenstaff so eloquently states in his Foreword, *The Success Factor in Piano Teaching* provides the rare opportunity to "sit at the feet of this remarkable teacher" as she addresses the most important topics in piano pedagogy.

In an informal and personal way, the reader will not only benefit from Elvina's expertise and insights but will also experience her unique and captivating personality — one which has engaged workshop participants and students for decades. The voice that speaks through these pages is one which will inspire, guide and challenge. To read *The Success Factor in Piano Teaching* is to experience time spent with a unique voice in piano pedagogy — one which communicates great wisdom, practicality, honesty, humor, and passion.

—Craig Sale

▲ PREFACE

The Success Factor in Piano Teaching is not a textbook designed for the purpose of presenting pedagogical guidelines for the achievement of success in piano teaching. Rather, it is a series of reflections, insights, and lessons which the author has learned about playing, practicing, and teaching piano during the past seven decades. Most of the book's contents are the outgrowth of actual "on-site" happenings which have provided invaluable information about what strategies work and which don't — especially in the area of teaching students how to practice, in order to achieve maximum success with minimum time and effort.

Although the book does examine in some detail the success factor as it relates to achieving a significantly high level of professionalism and pedagogical expertise, its primary focus is on practice. Consequently, nine of its fourteen chapters and nearly two-thirds of its pages are devoted to the subject of "making practice perfect."

The book's focus on practice is based on two premises: 1) that the primary purpose of the lesson is to prepare students for six days of productive, self-directed practice between lessons; and 2) that how students practice at home depends largely upon what goes on at their lessons.

The Success Factor in Piano Teaching identifies many of the common musical and pianistic issues that must be dealt with in practice, and it suggests ways to approach them both at the lesson and in practice. The "Practice Tips" which accompany the numerous musical excerpts provide step-by-step procedures for use at the lesson and also by the student at home. Ideally, these practice strategies will help to *prevent* problems from ever happening in the first place, but if they should occur, the "tips" will also be effective in helping to eliminate them. (It is recommended that readers study the "tips" sections at the piano in order to be able to actually "try them out.")

The author's long-term utilization of all of the book's suggested strategies in her own practicing, teaching, and performing has proven that her strategies really do work. Therefore, she is completely confident to guarantee their effectiveness without reservation to other pianists and teachers seeking solutions to similar problems. It is hoped that *The Success Factor in Piano Teaching* will not only be useful to those who teach piano, but also to those who play, practice, and perform at the piano just for the fun of it!

▲ INTRODUCTION

As stated in the Preface, much of the content of *The Success Factor in Piano Teaching* is generated by numerous happenings which I have experienced in practicing, performing, and teaching piano during the past seventy-plus years. Many of the opinions and conclusions which appear in the book were arrived at as the result of "real time" experiences which took place in the "school of hard knocks," maybe the best instructor of all. Cited below are names of some of the people and events that have significantly influenced both the selection and substance of the book's contents.

How did it all begin? . . .

My fascination with piano teaching began when I was in the fifth grade. One day, a friend of mine, Diane (who took piano lessons from the same teacher as I), told me that she was having major problems learning the pieces that she was being assigned and she asked if I would be willing to "coach" her a bit between lessons. I was intrigued by this idea and agreed to do it providing our teacher approved. She did, and thus, at the age of ten, my career as a piano teacher was off and running (although I didn't know it at the time!).

One afternoon a week Diane and I would go to her house, have a milk-and-cookies snack, and then adjourn to the living room where I would listen to her practice her assignment. It soon became clear to me that the major cause of her problems was not the pieces, but how she was practicing them. So I began to share with her some ideas about ways she might practice in order to achieve more satisfactory results with much less time and effort.

Diane seemed to like my ideas and she was a fabulous student because she actually followed through with applying the suggestions I made. We had a great time together, and both of us were happy with the results. *Could a "teacher" ask for anything more?*

For me, this experience with Diane ignited a keen interest in the subject of practice which, many moons later, was to become the main focus of this book devoted to finding ways to make practice more "perfect."

After Diane, what next? . . .

During my junior high and high school years, I added additional students to my roster. Unfortunately, unlike Diane, most of these students were neither eager nor willing to receive and apply my ideas. From these early teaching experiences I learned that not all kids liked taking piano lessons and that many of them hated to practice. Usually unable to generate enough student success to alter such negative attitudes, I soon became very aware of how much I didn't know about how to teach!

And so where did it go from here? . . .

Sensing my frustration, Helen Ringo, my piano teacher, allowed me to enroll in her piano pedagogy course at the University of Tulsa. (Incidentally, Richard Chronister was also a student in this same class.) Although somewhat after the fact, in this "pedagogy 101" class, I was at least beginning to get some useful ideas about both teaching strategies and materials.

Post-college studying and teaching . . .

After completing my studies at the university, it was off to New York to become a piano student of Isabelle Vengerova. (*More about this in the last chapter of the book.*) While studying in New York, I continued to teach, which entailed a weekly pilgrimage via bus and train out to Long Island and then walking from house to house to give the lessons. I spent more time traveling than I did teaching, and by the time I paid for my transportation, the earnings were virtually nil — but my ongoing fascination with teaching and what I was beginning to learn about practice-related issues more than made up for it. Both my NY Vengerova study and this teaching adventure are sources of still more material which appears in *The Success Factor in Piano Teaching*.

Post-New York study and teaching continues . . .

Upon leaving New York, I accepted a position on the piano faculty of Westminster Choir College in Princeton, NJ. An unexpected bonus was an opportunity to study piano pedagogy with the Chair of the Department — *Frances Clark*! This included her regular observation and supervision of my teaching as well as an opportunity to attend all of her collegiate lecture courses. Two of them, "Fundamentals of Piano Pedagogy" and "Practical Piano Pedagogy," subsequently became the foundation for an approach to piano teaching which, even today, strongly influences both what and how I teach. Needless to say, this too, has made its way into the book.

After Westminster and Frances . . .

I continued to work with students of all ages and levels, both independently as well as at Frances' New School for Music Study in Princeton; and some years later at North Central College in Naperville, IL, and at Northwestern University. All of these "live" teaching experiences have made me acutely aware of what piano students need to learn — especially about how to practice — in order to achieve the kind of success that will enable them to experience the joy of music-making at the piano. These needs are identified in *The Success Factor in Piano Teaching* along with specific "tips" for how to fulfill them.

Years of teaching piano pedagogy at the collegiate level have also informed me of the pedagogical needs of young people who might someday find themselves involved in professional music careers which will more than likely include some piano teaching. It is hoped that the contents of *The Success Factor in Piano Teaching* will be especially useful to such individuals.

And finally . . .

Numerous portions of this book were inspired by workshops which I have presented over a 50-year period in more than forty of our states, as well as in Canada, the Republic of China, and Australia. What a wonderful privilege and inspiration to meet and speak with the teachers who attended these events. Their participation in *Q & A* discussions at these workshops has played a large role in determining the issues which have been included in this book.

And speaking of workshops, I have certainly learned a great deal and obtained many wonderful ideas from all of the workshops which I have attended over the years. (I always feel rich when I leave one of these events with even just *one* new idea, especially if I know that I can use it that very day in my teaching!)

In conclusion . . .

It is hoped that *The Success Factor in Piano Teaching* will provide its readers with more than just one useful idea. In addition, perhaps it will also be a reminder of some effective teaching strategies which have been used in the past and probably ought to be revisited. To all readers of this book, I hope you enjoy it, and I extend to you many good wishes for your continuing success both as music makers and music teachers.

—Elvina Pearce

PART ONE:
PEDAGOGY

How We Teach

One of the definitions of "pedagogy" in Webster's *New World Dictionary* is "the art or science of teaching." Part One of *The Success Factor in Piano Teaching* is primarily devoted to a discussion of piano pedagogy which will be discussed from two points of view:

> *How* we teach,
> and
> *What* we teach.

Of course, learning *how* to teach is a lifelong study, and, in the final analysis, experience may indeed be the best teacher of all. However, we can also learn much about the components of good teaching by observing, reading about, and analyzing the methods of the most successful teachers. Aside from really *knowing* the subject and individuals whom they are teaching, what other basic pedagogical principles underlie their successful instruction?

▶ WHAT DO SUCCESSFUL PIANO TEACHERS KNOW?

Successful teachers know that:
- **teaching is <u>not</u> telling.**

"How many times have I told you that a half note lasts for two counts?"

"What does that *f* at the beginning of this piece mean? Didn't I tell you last week that *f* stands for 'forte' and means to play loud?"

"Today we're going to learn about whole notes. Here's a picture of a whole note. A whole note lasts as long as four quarter notes and gets four counts. Here's how we count whole notes."

Students learn not by being told but rather by discovering for themselves and *experiencing* the meaning of the concepts being presented. They learn on the basis of what they already know *(going from the known to the unknown),* and they learn best those things about which they really *need* to know. Therefore the most successful teachers are those who first of all create a situation in which their students have a need for whatever new information is to be presented, and then they create lesson events which will enable the students to *discover for themselves* those things that are important for them to learn.

Successful teachers know that:
- **to be thoroughly understood, each new discovery must be repeatedly used (experienced and drilled) in a variety of formats until it becomes a part of the student's habit.**

Successful teachers know that:
- **learning is growth.**

Growth is logical and natural, and is an inevitable, positive happening which occurs whenever a new concept grows out of an understanding of the concept that preceded it.

Here are three examples:

1. The student who has aurally experienced the concept of high sounds and can hear and produce sounds going *higher* on the keyboard then has a basis for understanding the concept of low sounds, and will know how to produce sounds going *lower* on the keyboard.
2. The student who understands the concept of the interval of a second—how it looks and sounds when played on the keyboard and how it looks when notated on lines and spaces—has a basis for understanding the structure of all other intervals.
3. The student who has acquired a strong physical sense of pulse related to a quarter note (can clap it, tap it, march to it, and play and count it) then has a basis for understanding and physically expressing its multiplication into half, dotted half and whole notes, and by the same token, its division into two eighth notes, triplets, sixteenth notes, etc.

Successful teachers know that:
- **understanding the "whole" should precede drilling on the parts.**

For example, before students are asked to write or memorize the key signatures for *all* of the major keys, they must first understand the structure of the major scale pattern and know that it is this pattern which determines whatever sharps or flats comprise a key's signature. This means that although a student might look at a major key signature and be unable to remember which key it represents, if she *knows* the major scale pattern, she will be able to arrive at the answer to this question. At the outset this may take a bit of time, but the important thing is that the student *has a way to arrive at the answer!*

A second example relates to learning the names of the lines and spaces in music notation. Asking students to utilize the *"Every-Good-Boy-Does-Fine"* and *"F-A-C-E"* method for learning the names of the lines and spaces on the treble staff bypasses the *reason* for their names — namely that the treble clef is actually the letter *G* and that its placement on the staff is what determines the letter names of *all* of the other lines and spaces. And the same holds true for the bass clef which is actually an *F.* Students who understand this concept, along with that of intervals, have a way to discover *on their own* the names and keyboard placement of any note on the grand staff as well as ledger line notes above, below, and in between the treble and bass staffs.

Successful teachers know that:
- **when piano students are really prepared, nothing is difficult for them to learn and demonstrate with security and authority at the keyboard.**

This being the case, it is the teacher's responsibility to get students ready to make each new discovery effortlessly, and then to be sure that adequate drill is provided for as long as necessary in order to ensure that each concept does indeed become part of the students' habit.

Successful teachers know that:
- **students learn better in an environment which is primarily "student-centered" as opposed to one that is "teacher-centered."**

The subject of how we teach should certainly include a discussion of the format of the environment in which we teach. From my perspective, one of the most important considerations is whether the lesson environment is primarily "teacher-centered" or "student-centered." As an illustration, here are several lesson scenarios.

Lesson Scenario Number One

In this example, the teacher informs the student — Steven — that today's lesson will begin with technique; she then sets the metronome at 60 and asks Steven to play the B-flat Major scale up and down, four octaves, playing four tones for every tick. After Steven finishes, the teacher says, "I thought that your tone quality and projection were very good; your rhythmic stability with the metronome was also quite good, and your fingering was accurate. However, I think your hand position does needs some attention. Your fingers were much too extended — not playing enough on their 'pads.' Because your thumb was not loose and flexible, I frequently heard accentuations whenever you played your thumb as it crossed under your hand in the crossings." The teacher then asks Steven to play the scale again and, this time, to think about his finger position and maintaining a loose, flexible thumb.

I would describe the above lesson scenario as being a "teacher-centered" approach. In contrast, here is another lesson segment — this one illustrating what I would consider to be more "student-centered."

Lesson Scenario Number Two

As in the previous lesson, the teacher asks Steven to begin by playing the B-flat Major scale, but before he starts, she says: "Before you begin, tell me three things that you are going to specifically listen for as you play." Let's say that Steven chooses *legato*, a full, rich tone, and staying with the metronome. Next, the teacher asks him to suggest two additional things for her to watch and evaluate as he plays, and let's say he chooses his finger position and thumb motion. Next, the teacher hands Steven the metronome and asks him to set it at the tempo he's been using for his scale practice at home during the past week.

When Steven finishes playing the scale, the teacher does not immediately jump in and evaluate his performance. Instead, she first gives him an opportunity to comment on it. What about the three things that he had chosen to listen for — *legato*, richness of tone, and staying with the metronome? And next, what about the two things that he had asked her to monitor (finger position and thumb motion)? Evolving out of this shared post-performance evaluation would be Steven's new goals and practice steps for the coming week's work on scales, and these would either be written on his assignment sheet or recorded on his audio/video device which he would listen to at home as a daily practice guide.

In the first lesson situation, Steven was simply a reactive participant, doing what the teacher asked him to do and then listening to her evaluation of his performance. In the second scenario, he not only participated in establishing performance goals before he began to play, but he also exercised an active role in the post-performance evaluation. I believe that students who are allowed to participate in this kind of "plan-play-evaluate" procedure at the lesson will be more apt to implement the resulting practice suggestions at home than they will those offered solely by a "talk-and-tell" teacher who does most of the orchestrating of the lesson happenings without soliciting much input from the student.

Here is another scenario which once again illustrates a more "teacher-centered" lesson environment.

Lesson Scenario Number Three

The teacher asks to hear Steven do a play-through of one of his "pieces in progress." At the end of his performance, the teacher says, "You've done some good work on this piece, Steven. I really liked the mood you created and, for the most part, I commend you on your accuracy. Now let's talk about what you need to do this week as you continue practicing this piece. There were some insecurities in the *RH* in those ascending passages in the first line. For instance, look at measure 3. I noticed that you were playing finger 3 instead of your thumb on the last *RH* 16th note in that measure, and you did the same thing in measure 4 on the fourth 16th note. I think it was this incorrect fingering that caused your stumbles in this passage. I'll circle the finger numbers here in your music to remind you to use your thumb on these two notes instead of finger 3. Now let me see you play just the *RH* of measures 3 and 4 again, this time using the correct fingering."

Continuing on, the teacher says, "In your performance, I also heard some hesitations in the second line. This happened because you are not yet secure with the *LH* chord changes. Let me show you how I want you to practice those changes this week." Etc.

Now once again, let's contrast this "teacher-centered" lesson approach with one that is more "student-centered."

Lesson Scenario Number Four

Let's suppose that as soon as Steven finishes his play-through of the piece, the teacher says, "Steven, what did you like about your performance?" And after he has answered that question, the teacher might also want to add a few other commendable things as well. Proceeding on, the teacher might say, "What things do you want to improve as you continue to practice the piece this coming week?" Hopefully, Steven would mention the stumbles in the upward *RH* passages of measures 3 and 4. Then the teacher might ask:

"What finger does the music suggest that you use on the last note of these two groups of 16th notes?" (*the thumb*)
"What finger did you use instead?" (*the 3rd*)
"Play that passage again slowly, first using the 3rd finger, and then repeat it using the thumb. Which is more comfortable?" (*using the thumb*)
"Why?" (*Because I don't have to stretch in order to be able to reach up to the next note.*)

The teacher agrees and then asks Steven to circle those finger numbers with a red pencil as a reminder of this preferred fingering.

Hopefully, in his post-performance evaluation Steven would also have mentioned his hesitations and stumbles between measures in the second line, and the teacher might ask:

"What happens there in the *LH* part that might have caused these problems?" (*the moves*)
"So what do you need to practice?" (*the LH moves*)
"Show me how you will work on these at home this week."

Notice here that the teacher says *"show* me," not *"tell* me."

In this fourth lesson scenario, instead of the teacher's pointing out the problems, the student was asked what *he* thought needed some attention and was then led to an understanding of what was causing the problems. Being aware of where the problems are and what is causing them leads to being able to determine the practice procedures that are needed to "fix" them. (Notice, too, that in this scenario, it was the *student* and *not* the teacher who did the circling of the finger numbers as well as being asked to illustrate the practice steps for the *LH* moves in line 2.)

Here are a few other general suggestions for ways to create a more "student-centered" environment which encourages students to become more actively involved in the lesson happenings:

1. Occasionally ask the student how he would like to start the lesson — with a technique warm-up? With theory? Or with a piece?

2. When assigning a new piece, sometimes play samples of several possibilities and then ask the student to choose the one she would most like to learn.

3. At the lesson, sometimes choose to hear a piece (or part of a piece) in progress, and ask the student to stop whenever a problem is encountered. When that occurs, ask the student to discuss what might have caused the problem(s) and then to demonstrate—*not* describe, but *demonstrate*—how he would work on that problem at home to solve it. Ask the student to summarize whatever practice strategies were arrived at, and these would then be listed in the assignment. *Of course these practice steps will only be meaningful if the student has done them and has experienced success with them at the lesson.*

4. With a *new* piece, after determining and marking its form, sometimes ask the student to take just one section and illustrate the practice steps that she would use when working out that part at home. Once again, the steps that the student *does* at the lesson are the ones that will be listed on the assignment or recorded for daily reference at home.

Successful teachers know that:

- **unless students experience success at the lesson with the suggested practice strategies, they will have little reason to ever do them at home.**

Finally, if we expect students to play an active role in effectively self-directing their home practice, they must also be given an opportunity to play an active role in orchestrating the actual happenings in the lesson itself. This suggests that instead of a large percentage of the lesson time being consumed with teacher "talk-and-tell," there should be a partnership between the student and the teacher which encourages student input and the exchange of ideas.

How we teach and the environment in which we teach are certainly laying the groundwork for our students, little by little, to become their own teachers until, eventually, we become *dispensable*. To the degree that this is happening, teachers can evaluate their pedagogical success.

Recommended texts

The brief discussion on the previous pages about what successful teachers know is but a mini-summary of a few of the basic fundamentals of teaching and learning which are presented and explored in depth in most collegiate music education and "piano pedagogy 101" courses. It is suggested that teachers who desire to review educational philosophy in more detail and/or explore more comprehensive discussions of piano pedagogy would profit greatly by studying the ideas presented in texts such as the following:

- *The Aims of Education and Other Essays* by Alfred North Whitehead (New York: The MacMillan Co., 1929).
- *The Art of Teaching* by Gilbert Highet (New York: Vintage Books, 1955).
- *Talks to Teachers* by William James (New York: W.W. Norton and Co., 1958).
- *Questions and Answers* by Frances Clark (Northfield, IL: The Instrumentalist Co., 1992; available from The Frances Clark Center for Keyboard Pedagogy).
- *A Piano Teacher's Legacy - Selected Writings by Richard Chronister.* Edited by Edward Darling (Kingston, NJ: The Frances Clark Center for Keyboard Pedagogy, 2005).
- *Intelligent Music Teaching* by Robert Duke (Austin TX: Learning and Behavior Resources, 2005).

What We Teach

Creating a student curriculum is surely one of a teacher's primary responsibilities. In addition to repertoire, it must at all times also include technique, theory, sight-playing, and creative work. Keeping all of these areas operative and in proper balance is often like a challenging juggling act for even the most experienced teachers. Without a doubt, skillful lesson planning plays an important role in assisting teachers with dealing with this challenge. The successful teacher usually constructs two types of plans: a *long-range* plan for the academic year, and a *weekly* plan for each individual lesson.

▶ LESSON PLANNING

Long-range planning

I think that the teacher needs to begin a new teaching year with at least a general plan for each student's curriculum. At the end of every school year in my own studio, I do a comprehensive evaluation of what each student has accomplished during the preceding nine months of study in the areas of musicianship, technique, theory, sight-playing, creative work, and practice habits. I also make a list of all materials assigned during the past year, noting which have been completed and which should be continued during the next season. In addition, I also list specific goals for the coming school year of lessons. These goals might be some of the following:

- to place more emphasis on imaginative, expressive playing, or on developing a wider range of dynamic contrasts;
- improving sight-playing; and
- in the area of technique, perhaps beginning the study of scale-playing or arpeggios; developing more technical evenness and clarity in the articulation of rapid passages; refining the execution of artistic pedaling.

I think that having specific goals such as these is essential as one contemplates the selection of materials to be assigned in the coming season of lessons.

Something which I have found to be both interesting and useful when making long-range plans for continuing study is comments provided by the students themselves in an annual end-of-the-year evaluation form. A sample of one of the questionnaires I have used to obtain their ideas appears on the next page.

The weekly lesson plan

It is my belief that a carefully constructed plan for the weekly lesson is essential in order to make the most of the limited amount of time a teacher spends with a student in the once-a-week private lesson. Such a plan not only establishes the order of the lesson's events but also includes both the new and review items to be assigned for the student's coming week of practice.

I have found that making a copy of each of the student's written assignments as they evolve during the lesson gives me an excellent starting point for planning next week's lesson. (For my copy I simply use old-fashioned carbon paper — yes, it's still being made, is inexpensive, and is available at most office supply stores.) A copy of the assignment not only provides a record of everything that was assigned for the week — both new and review — but also reminds me of the goals and practice strategies that were established for each activity and piece. I put an asterisk (*) beside anything that was assigned but *not* heard at this week's lesson and this serves as a reminder to be sure to check on this next week.

The weekly plan establishes the order of events that will take place at the lesson. The sample lesson plan provided on page 26 is for a junior high, intermediate-level student enrolled for a 45-minute weekly private lesson. (Because this plan is part of *The Success Factor in Piano Teaching*, it is explanatory in content and contains many more words than I would ever need to use in a plan actually used in the lesson. Usually the latter turns out to be just a brief skeletal outline of the order of lesson events, plus the materials to be heard and assigned or re-assigned, plus whatever important points need to be made with each.)

END-OF-THE-YEAR STUDENT EVALUATION FORM

DATE: _____

NAME OF STUDENT _____   Age_____   Grade_____

(Sept. _____) (Sept. _____)

1. List the three pieces (and their composers) that you liked the *best* this past year: _____

_____

2. Write the names of your two favorite books from this year: _____

3. List 3 pieces (and their composers) that you *did not like* this year: _____

_____

4. List any collections of pieces that you *did not like*: _____

5. How long do your parents think that you should practice every day? _____ minutes

6. How long do you think that you should practice every day? _____ minutes

7. How do you feel about practicing scales and other technique exercises?

_____ I like them _____ I don't mind them _____ I dislike them

8. What is your favorite kind of music? (Rate each category on a scale of 1 - 4, with "1" being highest.)

_____Music by old masters (Bach, Haydn, Mozart, Schumann, etc.)

_____Music by 20th century masters (Bartok, Kabalevsky, etc.)

_____Music by modern present-day composers (Olson, Rocherolle, Vandall, etc.)

_____Duets _____I like all of the listed examples equally well.

9. Name your favorite composers. _____

10. Name your *least* favorite composers. _____

11. What do you like *most* about group lessons? _____

12. What do you *not* like about group lessons? _____

13. Do you like making up your own pieces? _____Yes _____No

14. How do you like playing in piano programs? _____ I like it _____ I don't mind _____ I don't like it

15. What special kinds of music would you like to learn next year that you were not assigned this year? _____

_____

16. If your parents would let you, would you choose not to take lessons next year?

_____ I would not take _____ I'm not sure _____ I definitely would take

17. Do many of your friends take piano lessons? _____ Yes, many _____ No, not many   If "No, not many", why not?

_____

_____

SAMPLE LESSON PLAN
(for an Intermediate-Level Student)

1. Check last week's practice record and record the daily practice average. Also check the student's answers to the questions on page 2 of the last assignment sheet. (*See Chapter 13 for a sample assignment sheet.*)

2. Ask S (student) to choose the first activity – "Do you want to begin with a technical warm-up exercise or a piece?" (*It's interesting that when given this choice, almost all students usually elect to do some sort of a technical warm-up first. If the student gets to choose how the lesson will begin this week, then possibly I might determine this for the following week.*)

3. Hear a technique warm-up routine and assign a new one for coming week.

4. Hear a piece-in-progress. (*If I choose the piece, I try to pick one that I believe the student will play reasonably well so that the lesson can get off to a good start. If I ask the student to select a piece, it will usually always be one that he really likes and plays well.*)

5. Introduce a new piece — "Spinning Song" (*I always put the introduction of new material near the beginning of the lesson while the student is still "fresh" and in focus.*)

6. Hear "recap." of mvt. 1 of the Kuhlau sonatina. (Determine and list/record the new goals and appropriate practice steps for the coming week.)

7. Check on memorization of page 1 of Bach Minuet. (Assist with memorizing process as needed.)

8. Check last week's theory assignment (or other written work) and assign new.

9. Check sight-playing and assign new.

10. As time allows, hear all (or a portion) of one or more other pieces-in-progress. (List on today's assignment new practice steps and new goals.)

11. List on the new assignment sheet any additional materials to be begun or reviewed that were not covered in today's lesson.

12. End with a student performance of a sure-fire "winner!"

In summary

As previously indicated, each week's lesson plan, along with the copy I make of the student's written assignment, serves as the basis for my planning of next week's lesson. Although lesson plans are necessary, they are certainly *not written in stone!* As with the annual long-range plan, no weekly plan is ever "hard and fast," and teachers must be flexible and able to adjust it on the spot based on the lesson events and needs of the student. Even if it becomes necessary to make numerous changes in a lesson plan such as the one shown here, still, it is better to at least have it as a jumping-off point rather than to have no plan at all and instead use an "off-the-cuff" approach to teaching. The latter often is not only pedagogically ineffective, but also frequently results in a significant waste of lesson time.

Teaching the Beginning Student

As I think about teaching the beginning student, I am reminded of three related scenarios which I suspect will sound familiar to a number of you.

Scenario Number One

Not long ago an individual phoned to tell me that she had decided to begin teaching some piano students, and said she hoped that I would be willing to recommend her. As we spoke, she told me that she had never before done any teaching, but that she had had eight years of piano lessons when she was a child, and, therefore, she was sure that she could at least teach beginners. When I asked her what materials she planned to use, she was unsure but said that most probably she would just use the same beginning method books which she had used when she was a child.

Thankfully, this woman did not ask for my opinion of her decision to teach piano. And needless to say, I would *never* in a million years have recommended her! It's sad to realize that even though tremendous strides have been made in the field of piano pedagogy during the last half of the 20th century, there are still individuals who think that just because they had "x-number" of years of piano lessons when they were children, they are therefore qualified to teach. I think that what bothered me the most about the conversation with this woman was her conclusion that even though she was an inexperienced teacher, she could "at least teach beginners." (*Yes, and pigs can fly!*)

In today's world, there are so many educational opportunities available for individuals such as this person who are considering a piano teaching career. As starters, she could attend national conferences and teachers' workshops, join both a national and a local music teachers' association, enroll in a collegiate course in piano pedagogy (either as a participant or as an auditor), subscribe to music journals, explore the vast quantity of materials on display in browser bins at the local music store, audit private and group lessons taught by exceptional area teachers, and of course, she could also enroll for private study herself (either in piano or pedagogy or, ideally, both) with one of these outstanding instructors.

Scenario Number Two

This past year a mother brought her seven-year-old son, John, to my studio for a pre-enrollment interview. On the basis of his interview, I agreed to enroll him if this was her desire. I suggested that she discuss it with her husband and then phone me in a day or two to let me know what they had decided. She did call a few days later and said that because they had five children, they felt that they just couldn't afford the added expense of lessons for John. She went on to say that one of their older daughters — a fourteen-year-old who played both the cello and the piano — had agreed to teach him and that they thought this would work out just fine since John was only a beginner. *("... only a beginner". . . How I cringe whenever I hear this phrase. . .)*

Scenario Number Three

The quotation below probably describes the *modus operandi* of many parents who are seeking a first piano teacher for their child.

"I'm looking for a piano teacher for my eight-year-old daughter, Megan, who is a beginner. Since I'm not sure whether or not she has any talent, I've decided to enroll her with a neighborhood teacher and see what happens. Although I know that this person is probably not one of the leading piano teachers in our community, she's nice and the kids like her, her lessons are affordable, and it will be so convenient for me because Meg can just walk to her lessons. Of course if she shows interest and talent, then I can always switch her to a 'better' teacher later on if necessary." (*Alas! "Later on" may indeed be too late!*)

Here is what I wish I could say to this parent (and to all of the others who are looking for a first piano teacher for their child):

"I think that at this point, the most important 'talent' of all for you to consider is that of the teacher. And I think that the best way for you to find out if your child has any talent herself is to enroll her with the best educated, most experienced, and most talented teacher you can find!"

Without a doubt, I believe that the most important year of piano study for beginning students is the *first* one. I also believe that their most important teacher is the *first* one; and I believe that a student's most important piano book is also the *first* one. Because of this, I give to the parents of all of my prospective beginners the information contained in the essay which follows, hoping that it will provide some useful guidelines for choosing both a pedagogical approach and a teacher for their child when he or she is ready to begin piano lessons.

GUIDELINES FOR PARENTS OF BEGINNING STUDENTS

by Elvina Pearce

Although there are many different "method" books for beginning piano students in use today, almost all of them are based on one of two basic approaches — either *rote* or *reading*.

The Rote Approach

The primary goals of the rote approach are:

- to develop excellent aural skills (listening);
- to develop a high level of technical coordination, control, and facility; and
- to teach students how to play impressive-sounding pieces on the piano in a relatively short period of time.

In *pure* rote teaching, all of these goals are pursued *without* introducing the student to concepts related to note-reading. Students learn to play by watching and listening to the teacher's performance, and then by imitating what they have seen and heard. As reinforcement, many of them are also required to listen frequently to recorded performances of their pieces on a daily basis in between lessons. The merit of the rote approach is that students are unencumbered by the complexities of having to first understand and read notational symbols before translating them into sound at the keyboard. They are therefore free to focus all of their attention on reproducing the music they are exposed to. Thus, almost all children — even those of preschool age — can be taught to play fairly complex, impressive-sounding pieces in a relatively short time.

It should be noted, however, that success with an approach that is primarily rote is dependent upon parental attendance at all lessons and supervision of all of the child's practice. Parents should also understand that although a rote approach may produce students who play a "lot of piano" in a short time, it does *not* develop musical literacy — that is, the ability to read and translate music notation *with understanding* at the keyboard. Nor does it develop students who are acquiring the tools that will enable them to independently self-direct their practice. An additional concern is that the longer learning to read music is postponed, the more difficult it is apt to be for students to be willing to "back up" in order to acquire this skill.

The Reading Approach

Besides rote, the other basic approach to teaching beginners involves the presentation of reading music from the outset. In this category, there are two main ways to introduce reading. One is the traditional "grand staff" approach, and the other is via a "reading-readiness" approach. In each case, the student's initial pianistic experiences go hand in hand with learning how to read music notation. Thus, the acquisition of musical literacy is not postponed but begins at once.

• *Beginning with reading on the Grand Staff*

With the Grand Staff approach, the student's first pieces are written on the treble and bass staffs from the very outset. The downside of this method is that understanding even the easiest first piece notated on the Grand Staff necessitates the presentation of some eighteen different concepts — for example, the meaning of the two clef signs, time signatures, bar lines, line and space notes and which hand plays them, the correlation of up and down on the printed page with up and down on the keyboard, the names of the notes on the staff and their corresponding names and locations on the keyboard, dynamic indications, rhythmic values, counting, fingering, etc.

It is understandable that if young children are confronted with all of these concepts at the very first lesson, they can easily experience a considerable amount of confusion which frequently results in frustration. And this initial confusion is often compounded when more and more new concepts are added in subsequent weeks without allowing sufficient time for "internalization," and without students having the opportunity to read and play enough materials to reinforce them.

In addition, because the pieces in many beginners' books based on a Grand Staff approach advance in difficulty much faster than does the child's comprehension, much of the teaching of them ends up, out of necessity, having to be done largely by rote. This "rote" factor often produces a student who appears to be progressing rapidly through a method book of pieces which both look and sound "hard," but whose actual *understanding* of the basic principles underlying fluent music-reading is often quite deficient.

• *Beginning reading via the "reading-readiness" route*

The Grand Staff approach provides one way to begin music reading. A second way to begin it is via a "reading-readiness" approach. Here the goal is twofold:

1. to ensure complete comprehension of every principle related to the fluent reading of music notation.
2. to develop the ability to translate this understanding with technical security, control, and musicality at the keyboard.

Because of its emphasis on *understanding*, the reading-readiness approach often begins with pieces which use "off-staff" notation rather than lines and spaces on the Grand Staff. The purpose of off-staff notation is to prepare students, one step at a time, for each of the concepts related to Grand Staff reading rather than inundating them with all of this information at once.

Parents choosing a reading-readiness, off-staff approach for their child should be aware that at the outset, the student may appear to be progressing more slowly than do others whose pianistic skills may be developing at the expense of their becoming musically literate. Using a reading-readiness approach, it generally takes between a year to a year and a half for all of the basic notational fundamentals to be presented and thoroughly assimilated, but after this foundation-building period, the student is usually ready to forge ahead at a much more rapid pace than was previously evidenced. As a matter of fact, students may very well "catch up" with and even "pass" some of their peers who seemed to have been "ahead" of them during the first year or so of lessons. More importantly, when the primary emphasis during that first year has been on developing musical literacy and good practice habits, the student drop-out rate later on is apt to be much lower than it is for those students who have not become good readers and whose playing ability and practice habits continue to be largely dependent upon rote-teaching at the lesson and parental supervision at home.

Because I am thoroughly committed to the development of musical literacy right from the start, I use a reading-readiness approach with all of my beginners. But in the final analysis, regardless of the approach, a child's success is dependent primarily upon the understanding, interest, and support of his/her parents. This highlights the importance of parents becoming knowledgeable about the available approaches and "method" books for beginning piano study, and the need for them to carefully assess the goals and results of each of the options before enrolling their child for lessons. As a teacher, I feel a tremendous responsibility for what happens during a student's first year of study. I believe that it is the ***beginning*** experience that determines everything that is to evolve during subsequent years of study and growth, including a positive attitude about music and making music, both of which we hope will last for a lifetime!

In summary

In addition to providing the parents of all of my prospective beginners with the above information, I also discuss with them the first book that I shall be using with their child — a reading-readiness approach that begins with off-staff notation. At the interview, I show them the book and highlight some of its features. I also give them a chart summarizing the concepts that their child will have learned by the end of the first year of study.

Most parents find it pretty remarkable that a young child is able to assimilate and thoroughly understand this much material in just one year! But in addition to this, I want to be sure that they understand my most important priority — namely, the student's development into a complete, well-rounded, musically literate (and happy) performing musician. My role at all times is to maintain a balance between the understanding of concepts and the student's ability to perform what he/she understands with imagination, confidence, and with technical ease and security at the piano.

Hopefully all teachers who work with beginners are providing parents of their prospective students with enough information to assist them with making an informed decision about the criteria that should be used when selecting a first piano teacher for their child.

Teaching the Transfer Student

Quite possibly the most challenging and difficult aspect of piano teaching for many teachers is dealing with the "transfer" student — that student who comes to us having had some previous study with another teacher. Regardless of how well or how poorly the student has been taught, there are always two kinds of adjustments that both the student and the teacher must make — *personal* adjustments and *professional* ones.

▶ MAKING ADJUSTMENTS

Certainly in order to work well together, the personalities of both the teacher and the student must be compatible. Making whatever personal adjustments are needed in this area is usually fairly easy unless one or both of the individuals has some sort of psychological/emotional issues.

However, making *professional* adjustments can sometimes be a horse of another color, especially when it comes to standards. At the outset, the teacher will of course need to find out what the student's standards are for weekly lesson preparation and practice, and, by the same token, the student needs to get a clear idea of the teacher's expectations. Needless to say, the standards of the teacher and the student must be brought in line with one another before the two of them can settle into a comfortable and productive working relationship. This can sometimes take a considerable amount of time, depending upon the kinds of demands that were made on the student in his or her previous study. (I have found that it sometimes takes anywhere from a year to a year and a half before I feel that the student and I are actually on the "same page.")

Of course there is also always a period of adjustment between the teacher and the student's parent(s). To help with this adjustment, I always explore the following questions at the pre-enrollment interview:

- What are the parents' goals and expectations?
- How involved do they want to be? (Do they want to attend lessons, supervise the student's practice? etc.)
- What types of music do they want the student to play? (classics? modern? pop/jazz? hymns? etc.)
- Are they "contest-oriented?"

Even though these questions may have been thoroughly discussed at the pre-enrollment interview, once the lessons and the practicing actually begin, problems precipitated by parents can develop. For one example, I remember a little boy (age 7) who had had three years of previous study when he came to me for lessons. At his interview he played a movement of a Kuhlau sonatina and several other pieces of similar difficulty, and he played them all pretty well. (His mother told me that he had even won a trophy for his performance in a recent area piano competition.) However, I was stunned when I saw that in all of his studied pieces, a finger number and note name had been written in for every single note. When I tested his reading skills I was not at all surprised to discover that he could barely read even the easiest grand staff pieces in a first-year beginning method book. Obviously one of my main goals for him would have to be teaching him how to read music as soon as possible, and of course I discussed my plan for this with his mother.

The student enrolled, and, even though much of the lesson time was devoted to the acquisition of reading skills, I made sure that he continued to be assigned at least some music similar in difficulty to the pieces he had played at his interview. (Because of the level of difficulty of this music, we had to use a *lot* of rote and finger numbers to accomplish this.) For reinforcement of the concepts being presented in the area of reading, I assigned lots of written work and I also loaned him a book of beginning-level pieces each week for daily exercises in reading. On his assignment sheet, all of this reading material was always listed under the heading of "Review" even though it actually was not "review" at all since he had obviously never been previously exposed to it.

His mother attended his lessons, and, although she acknowledged that her son was making very good progress, especially in the area of reading, one day she confessed that the father (whom I had yet to meet) frequently made disparaging remarks to the child about "all of that easy *baby* music" he was playing. Even though the boy's attitude was wonderful, and his progress was very gratifying, it didn't take long for the father's negativism to spill over onto his son. And of course you know the "rest of the story" — his parents withdrew him after just a year of lessons with me (*and I never did get to meet his father!*)

This example illustrates that even though a student and a teacher may be making positive progress and getting along just fine, unless *both* of the child's parents are *100%* knowledgeable and supportive of the teacher's goals, standards, and expectations, it's a no-win situation with disaster lurking nearby. It is therefore important for the teacher to lay all of the cards on the table *before* the student is ever enrolled for lessons, and then to remain in fairly close contact with the student's parents during the transitional period — however long that might be. Having parents audit their child's lessons, or at least providing them with a frequent written progress report and a friendly phone update now and then, can help to keep things flowing in a positive direction.

▶ CHARACTERISTICS OF A TYPICAL TRANSFER STUDENT

Let me preface the following discussion by saying that of course, not *all* transfer students are fraught with multiple deficiencies and problems. Some of them have been extremely well taught. They are musically literate, play very well, and would be a joy to add to any teacher's roster. Unfortunately this is not always the case, and so in this segment, we are going to focus primarily on what I might describe as a more *typical* transfer student.

Below is a composite list of some of the characteristics of this "typical" student — let's say it's an eleven-year-old girl who has had four years of previous study. At her interview she plays a Bach minuet, the first two movements of the Clementi Sonatina, Op. 36, No. 1, and the "Spinning Song" of Ellmenreich.

The student's performance of these pieces reveals the following problems:

- numerous tempo fluctuations
- inaccuracies of both notes and rhythm
- poor tone quality and projection
- lack of dynamic contrasts
- much overlapping and blurring because of poor pedaling (in the 2nd movement of the Clementi sonatina)
- lack of technical facility, clarity, and evenness
- excess tension in the playing mechanism (in shoulders, wrists, elbows, etc.)
- poor positioning of the hands and fingers on the keys, and a weak arch
- virtually no balance between melodies and accompaniments
- lack of artistic shaping of phrase endings, etc.

The student's reading skills are tested and the following deficiencies were revealed:

- note-reading skills were several levels lower than the level of the performed repertoire
- student is better at reading notes on the treble staff than on the bass

- fingering and clef changes are ignored as are key signatures which determine the notes that should be sharped or flatted in the piece
- student has considerable difficulty reading ledger notes above, below, and between the staves
- student has no comprehension of intervals
- understands basic note values and rests (quarters, halves, dotted halves, and wholes) but does not read and play them accurately within the context of simple, early-level pieces
- has difficulty dealing with the division of quarter notes into eighths, sixteenths, and triplets
- does not deal accurately with compound meter
- has difficulty playing and counting aloud

In the area of technique:

When asked to play a scale, the student chose C Major (*of course!*), and played it hands together, up and down, two octaves, demonstrating:

- hesitations and stumbles because of errors in the fingering
- poor hand position with the fingers too extended and with virtually no supportive arch
- weak nail joints of the fingers which frequently caved in
- articulation lacking in tonal projection as well as clarity and evenness
- much unnecessary tension in the shoulders, wrists, and elbows

In music theory, the interview revealed that the student:

- had no knowledge of structural elements - things such as half steps, whole steps, major and minor five-finger patterns, triads and inversions, the major scale pattern, etc.
- had no knowledge of formal structure in music (ABA), etc.

About quality of practice:

On the basis of what was learned at the interview, this student probably does not do much slow or hands separate practice, and rarely counts aloud. More than likely, practice to her means just sitting at the piano for a prescribed length of time playing through the pieces on the assignment with little knowledge about what to do when problems are encountered.

Of course, the above list of characteristics is not to suggest that *all* transfer students have *all* of these problems, but my own experience confirms that all of them usually have at least *some* of them — even the cream of the crop — and many have more than just a *few* of them. Obviously in order to succeed with any transfer student, we, as teachers, must first of all find out specifically what the problems are and then find ways to overcome them as soon as possible. This latter subject could easily be the primary focus for a whole book. But in this one I do not intend to elaborate on what to do to "fix" the myriad problems that are encountered when teaching transfer students. Instead, my plan is to present some miscellaneous ideas that relate to this subject, and to suggest a few *do*'s and *don't*s which I have arrived at during my teaching career.

▶ A TRANSFER STUDENT'S FIRST LESSON WITH THE NEW TEACHER

One important big "don't" is to *never allow the student to feel that she is being demoted back to "easier" materials.* For this reason, I try to begin where the student *is* (or at least where she *thinks* she is). Therefore, the first few assignments will always include some material from one or more of the collections which the student had been using with the previous teacher.

Here is a suggested first week's plan for the assignment of a new transfer student.

Review pieces

From one of the student's previous books, ask her to choose two or three favorites to play at the next lesson. (These should be pieces that were not played at the interview.)

Technique

If the student has previously played scales, I'll ask her to select one to review. (If she has not studied scales, I would refrain from starting them at this first lesson because, at this point, this might consume too much lesson time. It also might not be one of the most interesting things to deal with, either at the lesson or in practice.)

In lieu of scales, I would assign some sort of a technique warm-up exercise (perhaps a 5-finger "rote" pattern that can be learned quickly and easily remembered, or maybe a Hanon study — but whatever it is, it should be something to be played rather than read out of a book.)

New repertoire

For most transfer students, I usually have selected at least one new book and/or a piece of sheet music, and I believe that it is best to start with one or two short pieces which can be taught and learned quickly rather than with one longer and more involved piece.

For most transfer students (and their parents), at the outset I try to select new pieces that:

1. both *look* and *sound* as difficult as those which the student has been accustomed to playing.
2. lend themselves to a good bit of "rote-to-note" teaching so that they can be learned quickly. (This is particularly necessary if the student is a poor reader.)
3. will sound impressive even if not played particularly well. (At this stage, I avoid assigning pieces that are sophisticated and filled with refined details, as is the music of such composers as Bach and Mozart, whose works generally require a first-rate artistic performance in order to be rewarding.)

In addition to the above new pieces, the student's first assignment will also include one additional new piece (ideally not more than one or two pages in length) which I choose from one of the previously used collections. This we will call an "on-own" piece which means that the student must learn it *all by herself* without any help from the teacher, or a parent, or anyone else. I ask the student how long she thinks it will take her to learn the piece (a week? two weeks?), and plan to hear it at the end of this period of time. This "on-own" piece usually always provides much useful information not only about what the student actually knows, but also about how she practices. It therefore usually serves as a perfect segue into the subject of how to practice.

▶ REMEDIAL WORK

Remedial reading
(note names, intervals, rhythms, fingering, dynamics, theory, etc.):

If a transfer student is a poor reader, we obviously need to be sure that we present all of the concepts which every beginner must learn, along with adequate amounts of written work and early-level reading pieces to reinforce them. At the lesson I tell the student up front that I have chosen very easy material because it's just for reading "review." (Here again, this material is not "review" at all since the student has never been previously exposed to it.) I also list all such remedial material under the heading of REVIEW on the student's assignment sheet. (*I've found that it's possible to get by with almost anything as long as we call it review!*)

Remedial theory

I do not consider the area of music theory to be a top priority for a new transfer student. However, the one thing which I think should be emphasized immediately is formal analysis of all new pieces, *i.e.*, how many parts does the piece have? how are they alike? how are they different? of what structural elements are they made?, etc. And the student would be asked to mark and label each new piece's form (ABA, etc.). Later on, after the student has made headway in overcoming the major deficiencies which were revealed at the interview, there is plenty of time to begin pursuing the addition of new concepts in other basic areas of theory.

Remedial technique

Another important "don't" relates to getting overly refined, detailed, and "picky" about technical issues too soon with new transfer students. I usually ease rather slowly into emphasizing this area since it is generally not a major turn-on for many of them. (*They want to play pieces!*) However, I will make some sort of a technique assignment since it can always serve as good "filler" for practice for those students who do not yet know how to use their time wisely.

After several lessons, I would probably begin to emphasize scale playing. If the student has not previously studied them, I start with the *Db* Major scale followed by *F#* and *B* Major. I choose these three scales because their fingering is so logical that it can be quickly understood and easily remembered. (These three scales all use all five of the black keys, played either with fingers 3-2 or 4-3-2, and in each scale the thumb plays the two white keys.) I also choose to begin scale playing with these three scales because even if students have had some scale assignments, more than likely, they have not yet played these three. (Note: *I never assign scales to be <u>read</u> out of a scale book.*)

Remedial practice habits

This is usually the area with which most transfer students need the most help. For this reason, my goal is to make sure that everything we do at the lesson prepares them for six days of productive practice in between lessons. In essence, I believe that a well-taught lesson actually turns out to be a supervised practice session. Of one thing I am sure — *whatever practice steps I want the student to do at home must be successfully done at the lesson*. I also know that it usually takes a *long time* for students to learn how to efficiently self-direct their practice, especially if they have already studied for several years *without* receiving significant instruction in this area. In the meantime, the more success they experience at the lesson as a result of using the suggested practice strategies, the more apt they will be to begin to employ them in their home practice as well.

One final "don't"...

I think that it is highly unprofessional for a teacher to ever imply that a transfer student has been poorly taught — not to his parents, and certainly not to the *student.* Rather, the focus should always be on the present — on our goals and on the progress which the student is making in every important area.

Teaching Students How to Practice

In this segment, the subject of teaching and practicing is approached primarily from the standpoint of the musical and pianistic needs of traditional ("average") students — the types of individuals with whom most of us spend most of our teaching time. Although much of what is discussed in this section about practice would certainly be useful to gifted "superstar"-type students as well, they usually seem to flourish and succeed in spite of how they practice (*and sometimes even in spite of how they are taught!*). But the success of average students probably depends more upon how they practice than on any other single factor.

 ## "TIME SPENT" VS. "MIND SPENT"

As stated in the previous chapter, I think that the primary purpose of the lesson is to prepare students for six days of productive self-directed practice in between lessons — practice that results in their ability to achieve maximum success with a minimum amount of time and effort. I think that for many students, instead of being "self-directed," practice is often "clock-directed." It consists primarily of just doing time at the piano, playing through the pieces on the assignment over and over again, often at too fast a tempo, and with little apparent knowledge or concern for what to do to achieve things such as accuracy, technical security, *a tempo*, musicality, memorization, etc. Hence, the status of the pieces being practiced often remains pretty much the same regardless of how long the student has been working on them or how many times they have been repeated.

Obviously, practice based on *time* spent rather than on *mind* spent — practice based on mindless repetition instead of the establishment of goals and practice strategies to fulfill them — at best produces only limited success which rarely results in positive attitudes about piano study. When we contemplate the kind of mindless repetition which seems to characterize the practice of so many students, one obvious conclusion is that they practice this way because they simply don't know what to do instead. This, of course, is where the teacher and lesson come into play. The things that students should be learning at their lessons about *how* to practice are the things that should be replacing the "mindless repetition" approach.

When I was a child, I practiced a lot, and I loved every minute of it. However, looking back on my practice in those early days and even up through my college years, I can't help but think of all the things I know now that I wish I had known then. Going a step further, what have I learned about the critical activity of practice that is easily teachable to my students? My annual summer assessment of their progress during the preceding year of study always includes a careful evaluation of their growth in terms of practice habits.

▶ "RULES OF THE ROAD" FOR PRODUCTIVE SELF-DIRECTED PRACTICE

Below are a few of the standards which I have established for effective practice. They're all things that I adhere to when I practice, and they're also all things which I want my students to understand and accept as "rules of the road" when they practice.

Establishing a regular practice time

Over the years I've found that I am more apt to practice if I schedule it to occur at the same time each day — granted, not easy, and not always possible, but if regular practicing is a priority (as it should be for all of us who teach), I've found it to be more possible than one might think.

The least satisfactory approach to practice is the "catch-as-catch-can" method. Those who utilize this approach often find that practice winds up being the last thing on their daily list of activities when perhaps they are too stressed out or just too tired to profit from it. This is especially true of students, many of whom are overly scheduled to the max. This is all the more reason for programming into their daily schedule a regular time for practice (*hopefully not at the end of a very busy day!*). I try to assist them with this process of choosing a regular time for their daily practice by recommending that they "try out" several possible times, perhaps before or right after school, or before supper, etc. For each possibility, I suggest that they practice at that same time for five consecutive days, and then at the conclusion of their "testing" period, they select the time that best fits their schedule (as well as that of the rest of their family). This, then, becomes their regular daily time for practice. Of course there will sometimes be disruptions in such a schedule but these should be exceptions — not everyday occurrences.

Doing several short practice sessions vs. one long one

I've also found that dividing my practice up into two or three short segments instead of just one long one is the best use of my time. I'm sure that this plan enables me to accomplish more because it makes it easier to approach each practice session with fresh endurance and concentration — both essential for optimum achievement.

I encourage my students to seriously consider the above plan and include it when they are "trying out" possible times for scheduling their daily practice. (It's my opinion that doing two 15-minute segments at the same time every day is often much more productive for many students than doing one 30-minute one.)

Although I know that not all of my students utilize these — practicing at the same time each day and dividing their practice up into several short segments — this does not negate the value of these two plans. I certainly do discuss the importance of both issues in much detail with prospective students and their parents at the pre-enrollment interview. And, in the beginning-of-the-year memo which is sent to each of my continuing students and their parents, I always remind them of the value of adopting the above two plans for home practice.

Analysis first when working out a new piece

For me, after doodling around a bit with a piece I want to learn, my first bona fide practice step is always to do a thorough analysis of the piece's structure. (How many parts does it have? How are they alike? How different? Structurally, of what elements are they made? etc.) It's analysis that actually reveals what and how much there is to practice. Analysis also provides valuable clues for which practice strategies would be most effective in order to learn the piece and be able to successfully perform it in a reasonable amount of time. In addition, analysis points up major considerations relating to musical interpretation, and provides the foundation for secure memorization.

Of course all students can certainly learn how to analyze a new piece. Ideally, this should happen at the first lesson with the very first piece, and then should be continued at every subsequent lesson whenever new repertoire is begun so that it indeed becomes a regular part of the student's practice procedures.

The "pencil" habit

I think that a pencil is an indispensable partner in practice, its use saving much time and often preventing initial errors as well as pointing up recurring ones. During my own "work-out" process with a new piece, I always mark and label its formal sections (ABA, coda, etc.), and I also pencil in things such as sharps, flats, naturals, fingering, sometimes even counting — whatever I think will help me learn that particular piece as quickly and thoroughly as possible.

I expect my students to also adopt the "pencil habit" in their home practice, and believe that this will happen sooner if, at the lesson, they actually do the marking of significant things rather than my doing it for them. Yes, this takes more lesson time, but in my opinion, it is well worth it!

Tempo selection

Another high priority in practice has to do with tempo choice. The standard I use for this when I practice is to always select what I call a "thinking" tempo — that is, a tempo at which I can see, play, hear, and evaluate everything that is happening. And I hold my students to this same standard both at the lesson and in their home practice. I believe it is folly to expect that accuracy, technical security, and even the goals of musicality can ever be achieved when much of one's practice is faster than one's current "thinking" tempo. To encourage students to choose a "thinking" tempo for their home practice, they are frequently asked to select their own tempos for performances at the lesson. Having done so, if problems occur, then the students themselves can realize that the tempo they chose was too fast and, with the aid of the metronome, they can reduce their speed until they finally arrive at a tempo at which they can successfully achieve whatever their goals might be. As students begin to learn that practicing at a "thinking tempo" not only produces success in a reasonable length of time but also drastically reduces the overall learning time for a piece, they are more apt to begin incorporating this strategy into their work habits at home.

Repetition in practice

Another important standard has to do with how one deals with repetition in practice. To be useful, repetition must always be purposeful. The following quotation is frequently attributed to Albert Einstein: "The definition of insanity is doing the same thing over and over again and expecting different results." In my own practice (*spanning well over fifty years!*), I have learned that it is usually non-productive to repeat something without first defining the reason for repeating it and then making specific changes in the practice strategies before doing so. And of course, this applies to my students as well.

As an example, let's suppose that at a lesson, the student is asked to do a "play-through" of a piece and hesitates or stumbles between measures 8 and 9. This being the case, why would the student go all the way back to measure one and repeat the whole passage again? Instead, a more useful approach would be to first understand why the problem occurred. In this instance, let's say that getting from measure 8 to 9 entailed having to move the RH to a different place on the keyboard and that it was insecurity with this move that caused the hesitation/stumble. This being the case, the student would first need to practice just this RH move until technical security was achieved. The next step would be to add the LH but to play only the end of measure 8 and over the bar line through the first beat of measure 9. When this is secure, then the student would backtrack a bit, playing all of measures 8 and 9, and finally, repeating the whole passage from measure one and continuing on — but of course being sure to choose a "thinking" tempo for this repetition.

It is obvious that repetition is essential in practice. Without it, no habits would ever be formed. However, it's *purposeful* repetition that makes practice productive. "Purposeful" means always having specific goals, and when problem-solving is an issue, it should involve:

1. identifying the cause of the problem,
2. knowing what to do to "fix" it, and then
3. DOING IT!

Multiple mindless repetitions played at too fast a tempo are rarely the answer. Knowing how to utilize purposeful repetition in practice is something all students can learn to do, but here again, they'll only learn this if they frequently experience it and the success it produces on a regular basis at the lesson. (*As an aside, I should emphasize that it is not just children whose practice is ridden with mindless repetitions. All one has to do to confirm this is to take a walk through the practice room areas of music buildings in collegiate institutions and one will hear exactly the same kind of repetitive practice occurring — but now it's being done by "gifted" piano majors instead of "average" kids.*)

Tackling challenges first

Another standard for my own practice is to tackle the challenges first. For me, this often entails beginning a practice session with the most challenging piece I'm working on, or with the most difficult spot(s) within a piece. I've found that this approach is usually more productive than postponing work on such a piece until later in the practice session. Approaching challenges with a "fresh" mind and ears, with alert concentration, and with abundant energy often works miracles. In addition, saving the less challenging pieces until later in the practice session is like treating oneself to a delectable dessert after completing the main course.

Again, students will learn the wisdom of this "challenges-first" approach very quickly if it is done frequently at the lesson. In addition, I often suggest on the lesson assignment sheet that this procedure be done at home with various pieces, i.e., "Don't start at the beginning. Instead, work first on the B part."

Working in short segments

Another strategy which I employ in my own practice is to work in short segments. Granted, playing through a piece from beginning to end is, at certain stages, an important part of practice because it allows one to measure endurance and concentration as well as to evaluate the current status of the piece — its overall technical security, memorization, musical interpretation, etc. However, when working on a piece (and students must, of course, always know the difference between working on and just playing through pieces), it is usually more productive to practice in short segments (say, 8-16 measures in length) rather than trying to plow through the whole piece, especially when utilizing a series of several practice steps. For example, if there are three practice steps — 1) RH alone, 2) LH alone, and then 3) HT — the student would do all three steps for mm. 1-8 prior to proceeding on to mm. 9-16.

Here again, if this "working-in-short-segments" approach is used frequently at the lesson and also specified in the assignment, students will be more apt to also utilize it in home practice.

Rotation of sections in practice

Because many students always start at the beginning of their pieces when they practice, the beginnings are often much more secure than the middle and last sections. In my own work at the piano, unless my goal is a "play-through" to evaluate where I am with a particular piece, I make sure that I frequently start my practice of all "pieces-in-progress" by sometimes playing the last section or the middle section first. For example, when practicing a sonata, I might one day begin with the recapitulation, and the following day, start with the development, etc. This ensures that these parts will have the advantage of receiving priority attention while I am still fresh and able to apply my best concentrated efforts in their behalf. This practice strategy results in the middle and ending sections of pieces being just as secure and convincing as the beginning.

Because of the time factor in lessons, I frequently apply this same principle, sometimes asking to first hear just the last section, or perhaps the middle section of a piece rather than allowing the student to always start at the beginning. If this "rotation" approach is utilized at students' lessons and specified on the assignment sheet, it will soon become part of their regular "bag of tricks" to use in home practice.

In summary

The above are some of the standards that form the basis of my own approach to practicing — things that I have learned over the years, and things that I wish that I had known when I was the age of most of my students. I've also learned that all of these concepts can be understood and applied in daily practice by all students, regardless of their age, level of advancement, or innate musical and pianistic ability. However, how soon, to what extent, and how consistently these strategies are implemented in home practice depends almost entirely on what happens at the lesson. Creating lesson situations in which students can repeatedly experience success as a result of utilizing intelligent practice procedures is of course one of the teacher's major responsibilities.

Early Level Repertoire — Tips for Teaching & Practicing

As previously stated, I believe that the primary purpose of the lesson is to prepare students for six days of productive self-directed practice in between lessons. If practice is to be effective, students must always leave each lesson with a clear understanding of two things:

1. *specific goals* for each piece or activity in the assignment; and
2. *specific practice procedures* for fulfilling them.

▶ BASIC STUDY GOALS FOR ALL PIECES

In my studio, the approach to all pieces, regardless of their level, is always based upon accomplishing the four basic study goals listed below. These consist of:

1. being able to play the whole piece 100% accurately and with technical security at a "thinking" tempo (this usually means *slowly*);
2. being able to play the piece *a tempo* with technical ease and security;
3. being able to convincingly express the musical "message" of the piece (its interpretation); and
4. achieving secure memorization. (Although memorization is certainly not required for all pieces, when it is, I see it as the fourth item on the students' list of basic study goals.)

I categorize all practice procedures designed to achieve things such as accuracy, *a tempo,* and technical security as "mechanical" strategies, i.e., things which most performers find necessary to do in order to get a piece ready to work on musically. All who have taught (or practiced themselves) would probably agree that nothing is more frustrating than trying to work musically on a piece which contains numerous inaccuracies and cannot be performed up to tempo with technical ease and security. For this reason, while students are in the initial phases of working out a new piece, I avoid making musical demands on them. This means that while they are in the process of doing whatever practice steps are needed to achieve goals such as accuracy and *a tempo,* I try not to muddy the waters by asking them to also focus on other things such as dynamic issues, balancing melodies and accompaniments, artistic shaping of phrases, pedaling, mood, tempo changes suggested by *ritards* and *accelerandos,* etc. There is plenty of time for dealing with all of these interpretative issues as soon as the student can play the piece accurately, *a tempo,* and with technical ease. When this is the case, then the performer is ready to shift the focus off of "mechanics" and onto *musicality* — the "good stuff!"

One of the most important determining factors in a student's ultimate success with a piece is what he or she does with it when first working it out. This is largely dependent upon the teacher's initial presentation of the piece at the lesson, coupled with the student's understanding and utilization of whatever practice steps are experienced at the lesson and assigned for home practice.

For an example, I am creating on the next pages an "imaginary" early-level student, "Mike", and let's suppose that at today's lesson I plan to introduce a new piece, "Fanfare in C" by Gurlitt. (This piece appears in *The Music Tree, Part 3,* of the *Frances Clark Library.* Distr. by Alfred Publ.; used with permission.)

Fanfare in C

Cornelius Gurlitt
(1820-1901)

▶ THE INITIAL LESSON PRESENTATION AND PRACTICE OF A NEW PIECE

I usually begin the presentation of a new piece by first discussing with the student what the piece is about and then playing it for him. (I do, however, make an exception to this "playing" policy with beginners. Because they are still in the process of acquiring reading skills, I avoid playing their new pieces for them until I know that they have read them. I want to be sure that they are actually *reading* and not just imitating or playing them "by ear.") After Mike and I talk about what a fanfare is and the instruments that often play it, then he's ready to hear it and then analyze it.

Analysis — always the first practice step

As I see it, the first practice step with any new piece, regardless of its level of difficulty, is to do a thorough analysis of the music. As I play the "Fanfare" for Mike, I'll ask him to follow the score as he listens, because after my performance I'm going to ask him some questions about it. The questions shown below will form the basis of his analysis of the piece.

1. Which hand has the melody? (*RH*)
2. The LH is made entirely of how many different intervals? What are they? (*3rds and 5ths*)
3. How many parts does this piece have? (*three*)
4. What letters describe the parts? (*At this point, I would ask Mike to mark and label the A and B parts as shown on the next page.*)
5. How is the B part like the A part? How different?
6. How is line two different from line one? (Circle measure eight.) (*The circle reminds Mike that only m. 8 needs to be practiced since it's the only one that is different from line one.*)

Based on our analysis, we would then determine what practice steps Mike should use at home this first week with the "Fanfare" in order to accomplish his first basic performance goal — being able to play the piece *100% accurately and with technical security at a slow "thinking" tempo.* The practice workout procedures which I would suggest for his first week of practice on this new piece are on page 60.

Fanfare in C

Cornelius Gurlitt
(1820-1901)

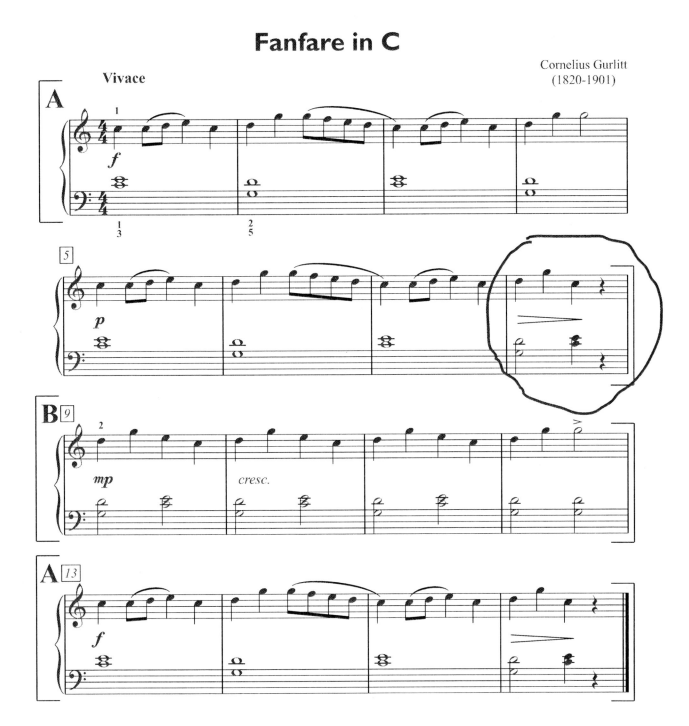

▶ PRACTICE STEPS FOR THE INITIAL WORK-OUT OF "FANFARE IN C"

1. **LH changes (play the two intervals 2-3 times, listening for legato)**
   (If Mike has difficulty connecting the two intervals, I would ask him to play just the top two notes legato — E to D with fingers 1 and 2 and just the bottom 2 notes legato — C to G with fingers 3 and 5. When easy, then he would play the two intervals as written, listening for legato.)

2. **RH - play/count**
   (I always ask students at this level to do a "count off" of at least one measure before beginning to play and count the piece. Since there are eighth notes in "Fanfare," in order to ensure the proper relationship between quarter and eighth notes, the count-off would have to include them. So Mike would choose a "thinking" tempo, a slow one, and then count "1-uh, 2-uh, 3-uh, 4-uh," which should segue without a pause right into the actual playing and counting of the RH.)

3. **Together-notes *only***
   (At this early level, many students have difficulty coordinating the two hands when they play together. If this is the case with Mike, I'll ask him to play just the together notes prior to adding the notes in between. So without any rhythm, he will play only the notes indicated with the vertical lines shown in the example on the next page. I've found that this "together-notes only" practice step greatly assists students with the coordination of hands-together playing.)

4. **HT (hands together) as written. COUNT!**

Of course, these four practice steps will either be written on Mike's assignment sheet, on his music, or recorded on his audio or video recording device which he brings to every lesson. At the lesson, I would ask a student at this early level to do at least a bit of all assigned practice steps (perhaps with just the first few measures of the "Fanfare") to be sure that he understands and has successfully experienced them prior to beginning his home practice of the piece.

Of one thing we can be sure — we can never expect students to do anything at home that they have not successfully done at the lesson!

Fanfare in C

Cornelius Gurlitt
(1820-1901)

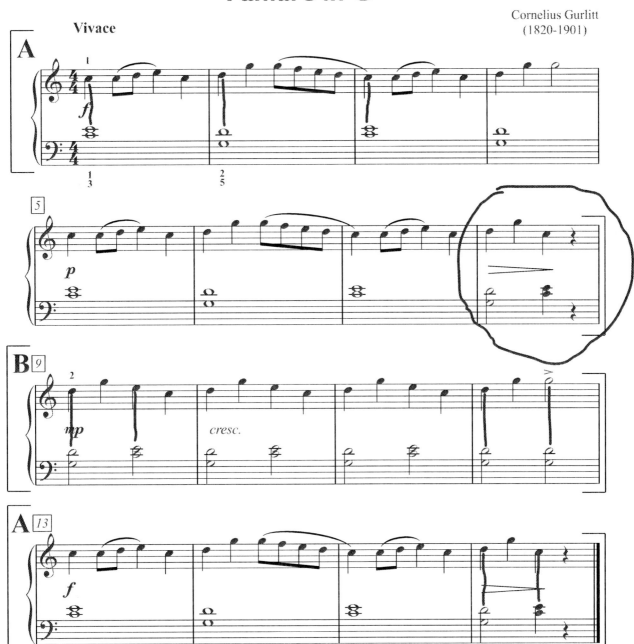

Achieving a tempo

Mike knows that his first basic study goal with any new piece is to be able to play it 100% accurately and with technical security at a "thinking" tempo. (For the "Fanfare" this might be around ♩ = 72).

(I would expect a traditional "average" student who uses the above practice procedures to be able to achieve this first study goal by the end of one or two weeks of practice.)

As soon as Mike can demonstrate his ability to perform the piece securely at a slow tempo, then he is ready to focus on study goal number two — achieving the appropriate performance tempo (perhaps around ♩ = 120). Here are two different practice strategies that he might use to arrive at this tempo.

Strategy #1

(Increase tempo incrementally)
1. In line 1, play *RH* alone at these 3 metronomic tempos:
   first slowly at ♩ = 88;
   then at ♩ = 104;
   and finally at ♩ = 120.
2. Play line 1 *HT* at the same three tempos.
3. Do steps one and two with the 2nd line and then with line 3.
4. Play whole piece at the suggested performance tempo.

Strategy #2

(Increase tempo via "impulse" practice)
1. At ♩ = 120, play *RH* of measure 1, stopping across the bar on the first note of measure 2.
2. Play *RH* of m. 2, stopping across the bar on the first note of m. 3, and continue on with the same procedure (playing each measure + the first note of the next measure) for the first 8 measures.

etc.

3. Same as steps 1 and 2 but *HT*.

As soon as a student can do the above impulses of a measure + 1 successfully, I would then assign the same procedure with impulses of two measures + 1, then four measures + 1, etc., until he is able to play the whole piece, nonstop, *a tempo*.

I think that when students have difficulty playing *a tempo* in "fast" pieces, it is not so much because of technical deficiencies but rather because of lack of mental focus and concentration. Although the "impulse" practice strategy described above does entail playing *a tempo* at once, because students start out with very short impulses, they are able to achieve immediate success. By gradually lengthening the impulses, they are also gradually expanding their concentration span and thus are acquiring the mental endurance necessary for staying "in focus" for the duration of a whole piece. In a nutshell, it's not just the fingers that must be trained to *play* fast — it's also the mind that must be programmed to concentrate and *think* fast — and to be able to do so for an extended period of time.

▶ FOCUSING ON MUSICAL INTERPRETATION – THE GOOD STUFF!

Once Mike has achieved study goals one and two with "Fanfare" (accuracy at a *slow* "thinking" tempo, followed by *a tempo)*, then he's ready to devote all of his attention to the third basic study goal — expressing the piece's musical message, its interpretation.

Because "Fanfare" is a pretty straight-forward piece, its musical considerations primarily have to do with executing the dynamic changes (*f, p, mp,* and *crescendos* and *diminuendos*), plus a couple of melodic accents appearing in mm. 4 and 12. In addition, the student needs to know the meaning of *vivace*.

(As soon as students begin playing pieces which contain musical terms such as "vivace," I ask them to purchase an inexpensive music dictionary. Whenever a new word appears, I don't tell them its meaning. Instead, it is their responsibility to look it up and then write its definition right onto the music itself.)

Dynamics

At the lesson, I would ask Mike to first circle the dynamic cues in lines 1, 2, and 4, and then play the first two lines, listening for the echo effect of the change from *f* to *p*.

Line 3 suggests a *crescendo* from m. 10 up to m. 13. Executing a *crescendo* over a span of several measures is not easy for most early-level students. To be able to effectively do this requires dealing with what is generally referred to as "terraced dynamics," i.e., increasing the volume by segments rather than trying to do it on a note-by-note basis.

When working with Mike on dynamics in "Fanfare," in line 3, I would first of all suggest starting this line *pp* rather than *mp* as indicated. Then I would pencil in a "*p*" for m. 10, an "*mp*" for m. 11, and an "*mf*" for m. 12 which leads directly into the *f* in line 4.

After penciling in the suggested dynamic cues for mm. 9-12, I would then ask Mike to play each measure, stopping in between measures in order to evaluate the dynamic level just produced, and also to plan for the following measure's dynamic change. Finally, he should play the whole line nonstop, and *Voila!* — a mini crescendo should be there. Of course I would illustrate this process as we discuss it to ensure that Mike will have a model for the desired sound in his ear before he is asked to produce it himself. (*A piece like "Fanfare" provides a wonderful opportunity to prepare students for dealing with terraced dynamics in more advanced pieces such as the Grieg "Nocturne" which is discussed in Chapter 8.*)

The last practice step would of course be to play the whole piece, listening for the desired dynamic changes. "*Did my playing match my plan?*"

Memorization

If "Fanfare" is to be memorized (goal #4 of the "Basic Study Goals" listed at the beginning of this chapter), Mike's initial analysis of its form (seeing what's alike and what's different), and structural elements plus his work-out of the piece should make it very easy to fulfill this goal.

(As teachers, what we need to be sure of is that our students know that the route to secure memorization is always based on an understanding of structure and never on just the "finger memory" which results from playing a piece over and over again!)

Because of his initial analysis of "Fanfare," as he memorizes, Mike should be aware that:

- Line 2 is exactly like line 1 except for m. 8
- Line 4 is exactly like line 2 (except for the *p* and *f.*)
- In line 3, mm. 10 and 11 are exactly like m. 9.

The following practice steps will help Mike achieve secure memorization of the "Fanfare."

Practice steps for memorization of "Fanfare in C"

1. Play mm. 1-4 two times -
   first, looking at the notes
   then cover the music and play one time without looking.
   (Note: *Step one could be broken down into shorter segments — say, two measures each — and also done hands separately if necessary.*)
2. Repeat step # 1 with lines 2, 3, and 4.
3. Play whole piece, one time looking at the music and then repeat it without looking.

In summary

You recall that when I first introduced our imaginary student, Mike, I categorized him as a traditional "average" student. Assuming that this is the case, I would therefore expect that he would be able to fulfill all four of his basic study goals with "Fanfare" (accuracy, *a tempo*, musicality, and secure memorization) in 3 to 4 weeks or perhaps even sooner, providing he has understood the suggested practice steps, experienced success applying them at the lesson, and has also utilized them in his practice at home.

▶ A FEW MORE WORDS ABOUT MEMORIZATION...

Playing from memory in public performances first began in the 19th century. At the time, it was the cause of much controversy and interestingly enough, in this 21st century, the debate about the virtues of playing without the music versus playing *with* it rages on.

The history of the practice of performing from memory is fascinating. One interesting anecdote cites the story of Sophie Bohrer, a young child prodigy of the 19th century. In *A Dictionary of Pianists and Composers for the Pianoforte* (Novello, Ewer & Co., 1896), Emil Pauer tells us that for a piano concert in Vienna, little Sophie's program contained a list of some 80 of the longest and most difficult compositions in the pianist's repertoire, each of which she professed to be able to play from memory at the audience's request.

Famous pianists and pedagogues from all over Europe were invited to attend this event, and at the concert they were asked to randomly select pieces from "Sophie's list" for her to perform without the music. She is said to have presented a flawless performance of each! Unfortunately however, this story does not have a happy ending, for it is written that shortly after this event, little Sophie disappeared from the concert world and never resurfaced. She reportedly was suffering from a chronic case of severe nervous instability.

Speaking of nerves, it is recorded that Clara Schumann (said to be among the first concert pianists to publicly perform from memory), suffered from severe anxiety because of this practice. In an 1871 letter to Brahms, she wrote, "God knows how I can begin to control the anxiety that is attacking me… I am often so nervous from one piece to the next, (that) I cannot make the decision to play without the notes." With age and heavy responsibilities, Clara found playing from memory increasingly difficult and thus, she eventually abandoned the practice. (Apparently this decision did not in the least affect her popularity as one of the most beloved and sought-after concert pianists in Europe.)

Actually, Sir Charles Halle is the person credited with starting the practice of performing from memory. In 1861, he presented a series of recitals featuring the 32 Beethoven sonatas, *all* performed from memory. We are told that, although audiences of that day were stunned by such feats, music critics did not applaud this practice, considering such undertakings as hazardous musical experiments, and likening them to the antics of trapeze artists in a circus. They further suggested that audiences came to concerts more to witness the downfall of the performer attempting to play from memory than to experience and enjoy the music being made. Nonetheless, in spite of the critics, the practice of playing from memory flourished in the 19th century, and virtuoso Franz Liszt stood at the head of the class.

When I was a student in New York, I fondly remember attending every Carnegie Hall recital of Dame Myra Hess for which I could get tickets, and I recall that Dame Myra usually appeared on stage with both her music and her page-turner. What heavenly music she made! And who would dare to suggest that it would have been even more so had it been played from memory!

I'm sure that most concertgoers could also cite superb recitals that they have attended in which the performer(s) used the music. All of this simply illustrates that whether or not performers play with or *without* the music doesn't seem to have much, if any, effect on the overall quality of their performances.

Be that as it may, I suspect that there will always be people ready (and even eager) to debate this issue at the drop of a hat. Apropos of this, I recall that some years ago, there was an excellent article in *Clavier* magazine (which became *Clavier Companion* in 2009 after a merger with *Keyboard Companion*) questioning the need for performing from memory. As a result, in subsequent issues of the magazine, there continued to appear numerous letters to the editor from readers speaking in behalf of the necessity for performing from memory as well as letters from others who defended the practice of performers using the music if they chose to do so.

And even today, the controversy continues. From my own point of view, I never have bought into the belief that performers necessarily play or sing better when they do so without the music. Instead, I contend that the primary issue should always be the quality of the musical performance rather than the format of its presentation.

Thinking in terms of the performances of children — particularly those who might be categorized as traditional "average" piano students such as our imaginary student, Mike — it is my belief that they should be allowed to use their music in informal studio recitals if they feel more comfortable doing so. Consequently, they will be apt to play better and experience more pleasure when sharing their music-making with others. Above all, I believe that at public recital events which are attended by mom and dad, grandma and grandpa, Aunt Susie and Uncle Joe, along with the performers' siblings and friends, it is *essential* that students be successful — they must be able to shine like the brightest stars. If using the music enhances and ensures their success at these important "recital" events, so be it!

On the other side of the coin, I also believe that *all* students should learn to memorize — but not just so they can perform in a recital or a contest without the music. From my point of view, memorizing is important primarily because of the residual benefits that this mind-stretching activity can provide — learning how to focus and concentrate being among them. I also think that students should have frequent opportunities to perform from memory — just not necessarily in a public recital. Regularly scheduled group lessons, performance classes, and even the occasional overlapping of two private lessons can provide great opportunities for them to try their "memory wings" in an informal, friendly and non-threatening environment provided by their peers.

All of my students perform in at least two informal piano programs a year. I leave the choice of whether or not they play from memory entirely up to them and they almost always make a wise decision.

References
Thorpe, L. P., & Whistler, H.S. (1964). Memorizing Piano Music. In R. Savler (ed.), *The Piano Teacher* (pp. 10-20). Evanston, Il: Summy-Birchard Co.

Technique — Tips for Teaching & Practicing

In my opinion, one of the best books ever written on the subject of teaching and practicing piano technique (and one which I think all teachers and pianists should own) is *The Art of Piano Playing* by George Kochevitsky. (Originally published by the Summy-Birchard Co. in 1967, the book is currently available through the Alfred Publishing Co.) In his book, Mr. Kochevitsky says this about technique: "Piano technique, in a broad sense, is the sum of all of the means a performer has for realizing his purpose, his artistic musical idea." (p. 36)

I think that most musicians would agree with Mr. Kochevitsky's definition of "technique" and would concur that the primary purpose of pursuing its development is to acquire a means for communicating the expressive intent of a piece of music.

Apropos of teaching and practicing technique, there is one school of thought which believes that most of the skills pianists need to possess can be acquired by practicing exercises apart from pieces of music, i.e., Hanon studies, 5-finger exercises, scales, arpeggios, chords, octaves, trills, etc. Another school of thought claims that we really don't need to practice such exercises. Instead, all we need to do is to extract specific technical elements from the pieces of music we are studying and then create and practice technical exercises made out of them. Probably most teachers and performers fall into a third category, believing that utilizing *both* approaches is the best route to acquiring a well-rounded, effective keyboard technique. I personally think that, for most of us and our students, one approach without the other would be insufficient.

In this chapter, we are going to discuss the development of technique from both standpoints:

> *Making and practicing exercises derived from technical challenges found within the music itself,*
> and
> *Practicing exercises apart from music.*

As we proceed, it is well to keep in mind that regardless of how one approaches the development of technique, the ear must always be the key factor in its practice. It's the ear that must continually set our standards for the desired sound and then evaluate the results of our efforts.

▶ PART I: DEVELOPING TECHNICAL SKILLS VIA EXERCISES DERIVED FROM THE MUSIC ITSELF

Many early-level pieces require technical skills which may be relatively new to a student. As stated in the previous chapter, I classify all of these skills as part of the "mechanics" necessary for achieving 100% accuracy with a piece so that the performer is then free to focus on its musical interpretation. Whenever music contains technical challenges, students need to know how to deal with them in their practice. (Of course *these are the things they should be doing at the piano instead of succumbing to the mindless, repetitious "play-through" approach* to practicing that was described earlier.)

As an example, in "Fanfare in C" we discussed how our imaginary student, Mike, might work on coordinating hands together by first playing only the together notes of that piece before adding the notes in between. We also discussed a way he could practice the *LH* intervals in order to be able to achieve *legato* connections.

Below are some other technical challenges that students will undoubtedly find in their repertoire and with which they must know how to deal in their practice. Whenever a piece contains elements that will probably need special attention, I create exercises out of them and assign them to be practiced as "warm-ups" prior to starting actual work on the piece itself. Each repertoire excerpt which follows is accompanied with tips suggesting ways to deal with the technical challenges via practice warm-ups.

Sustaining notes in one hand vs. playing staccatos in the other hand

In Türk's "March in C," the student has to be able to sustain the *LH* whole notes while simultaneously playing staccatos in the *RH*. (This piece is found in *The Music Tree, Part 3*, from the *Frances Clark Library*; Dist. by Alfred Publ. Co; used with permission.)

March in C

Daniel G. Türk
(1756-1813)

Brightly

PRACTICE TIPS

1. When the student is ready to put the two hands together, at the lesson I would ask her to first play
    only the "together" notes in measures 1, 3, 5, and 7, holding down the *RH* and *LH* "together" notes
    for counts 1 and 2 and then releasing the *RH* note on count 3 while continuing to sustain the *LH*
    whole note during counts 3 and 4.

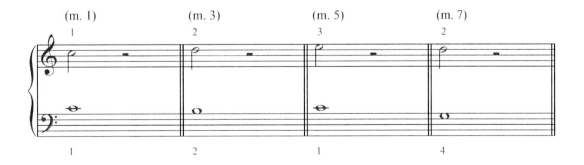

2. When tip number one is easy, play the "together" notes again, but this time, release the *RH* on count 2 while holding the *LH* note for all four counts.

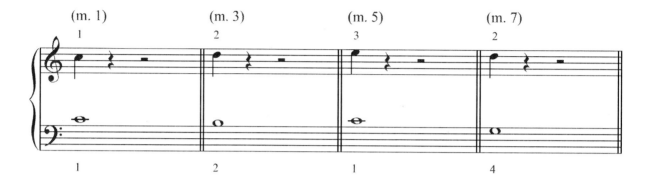

3. Next, play *HT* as written but very slowly, listening for the release of the *RH* staccatos vs. the sustained *LH* whole notes.

I would recommend that before students attempt to play the whole piece HT as written, they first do steps 1 and 2 as preparatory warm-up exercises for at least one week.

Balancing melodies and accompaniments

The Diabelli "Bagatelle" requires that the *RH* melody project over the *LH* accompaniment — usually not an easy thing for early-level students to be able to do. (The "Bagatelle" appears in *Keyboard Literature, Part 3,* of *The Music Tree.* Dist. by Alfred Publ. Co., used with permission.)

Bagatelle

With Motion

Anton Diabelli
(1781-1858)

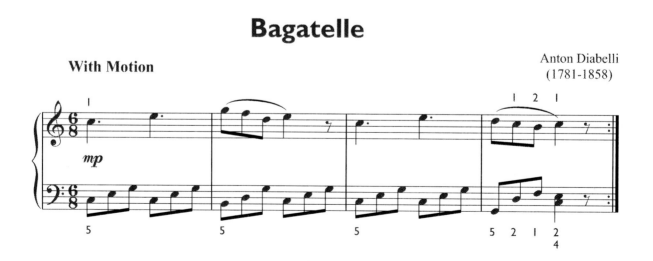

PRACTICE TIPS

1. At a very slow tempo (♪ = 60 or even slower if necessary), play the *RH* melody *mf* and super *legato* while playing the *LH* accompaniment *pp* and detached.

2. Repeat the process several times, gradually increasing the tempo.

3. Play the piece *a tempo* as written (♪ = 144), but this time, play the *LH* accompaniment *pp* and *legato* as written.

A more difficult and sophisticated intermediate-level piece which requires the artistic balancing of melody and accompaniment is "Sweet Dream" from Tchaikovsky's *Album for the Young,* Op. 39.

Sweet Dream

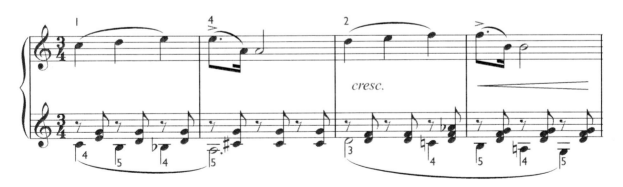

In analyzing this piece, the student should have discovered that in the A part (the first 16 measures), there are two melodies to deal with — one in the upper voice, and one in the lower (indicated by the down stem notes). The accompaniment is in the middle and supplies the harmony. The following are suggested practice steps for this section of the piece.

PRACTICE TIPS

1. Play the *RH* melody notes alone *mf*.

2. Play the down stem *LH* melody notes alone *mf*.

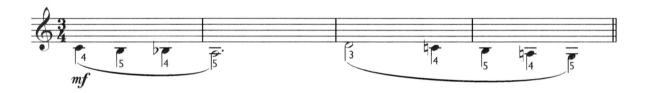

3. Play both the *LH* and *RH* melodies together, omitting the inner accompaniment.

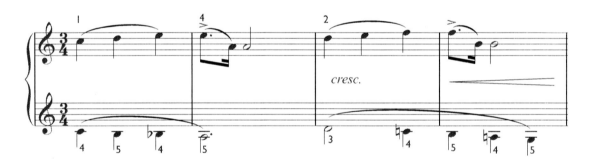

4. Play the *LH* melody (down stem notes), *mf* and *legato*, plus the accompaniment (*LH* upstem notes), *pp* and detached.

5. Play the *RH* melody *mf*, plus the *LH* up stem harmony notes, *pp* and detached.

6. Play all parts as written, listening for the two melodies to sing out over the *pp* accompaniment.

At the lesson, we would probably only do the above practice steps with a couple of measures just to be sure that the student understands and has successfully experienced them prior to beginning her home practice of the piece

Voicing chords

Students must also know how to practice in order to voice chord tones within one hand. Tchaikovsky's "Morning Prayer" is an example of such a piece. (It appears in *Piano Literature, Book 5b*, of the *Frances Clark Library*. Dist. by Alfred Publ. Co. Used with permission.)

Morning Prayer
from the "Album for the Young," Op. 39

Peter Ilyitch Tchaikovsky

Let's assume that the student wants to project the upper tones of the *RH* chords. The practice suggestions below will help him learn to do this.

PRACTICE TIPS *(to begin as soon as the student can play the piece securely as written).*

1. Play only the upper melody notes of the *RH* part. Play in rhythm, *mf*, and as *legato* as possible, using the suggested fingering.

2. At ♩ = 60, play the *RH* upper melody notes plus the lower bass tones, still *mf*, *legato*, and without the pedal.

3. Play the upper *RH* melody *mf* and *legato* and the lower *RH* tones *pp* and detached.

4. Repeat step #3 but add the *LH* part, also playing it *pp* and detached.

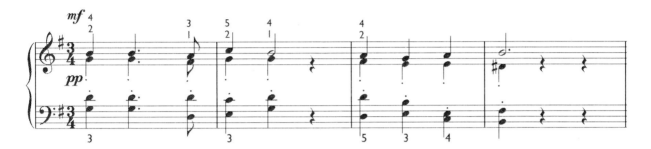

I would suggest that a student continue to do the above practice steps each day with a short segment of the piece prior to playing the piece as written.

5. Play *HT* as written with the addition of pedal.

Achieving evenness and clarity in rapid passages

With most students, a considerable amount of attention needs to be given to achieving technical evenness and clarity, especially when playing rapid passages. The "Arabesque," from Burgmüller's Op. 100, provides an excellent opportunity to develop such skills when playing consecutive sixteenth notes.

Arabesque
Op. 100, No. 2

Johann Burgmüller
(1806-1874)

Whenever I assign a piece such as the "Arabesque" I always ask the student when practicing to first do a 5-finger "warm-up" exercise such as the one below.

5-FINGER WARM-UP

1. Play each hand alone – 1x.
2. Play HT – 1x.

Practicing Chords

In the student's initial workout of the "Arabesque," he would have been asked to circle each *changing LH* chord as shown in the musical excerpt below. Using the "play-prepare" strategy (see "Practicing Octaves" discussion later in this chapter), he would then practice just the circled *LH* chord changes.

With many students, *LH* chords such as these in the "Arabesque" will also need some additional attention.

Because the 5th finger is a short one, the hand is often not properly balanced for executing all three notes of the chord simultaneously and, consequently, we frequently do not hear the bottom note of the *LH* chords. When this is a problem, I ask the student to practice the *LH* alone as shown in the following examples.

1. Play just the bottom and top notes of *LH* chords.

2. Play just the bottom and middle notes of *LH* chords

3. Play just the middle and top notes of *LH* chords.

PRACTICE TIPS (*before* playing the piece *HT* as written)

1. *HT*, at a moderate tempo, play the *RH* as written and play only the *LH* 5th finger along with it.
2. *HT*, play *RH* as written and play only the bottom and top notes of the *LH* chords.
3. *HT*, play the *RH* as written and play only the bottom and middle notes of the *LH* chords

The final step would be to play the piece as written, hands together, at a moderate tempo, listening especially for the bottom note of each *LH* chord.

Achieving evenness and clarity in repeated passages

Starting at the early-intermediate level, students will probably begin to encounter repeated bass passages such as those which occur in much sonatina literature (Alberti basses, etc.). These are usually found in the *LH* part, and being able to articulate them with clarity and evenness often provides another technical challenge for many students. The example below is from Kuhlau's *Sonatina,* Op. 55, No. 1 (mm. 17-22), and is typical of such patterns.

Whenever I assign a piece that has patterns of this sort, I always assign warm-up drills to be done daily before the student begins to practice the piece *per se.* The following examples illustrate several such drills.

PRACTICE TIPS

1. Block the *LH* chord changes.

2. Practice in "accents" of 2's, 3's, and 4's.

a. In 2's: accent every other *LH* note ($\quad$ = 58)

b. In 3's: accent every 3rd *LH* note ($\quad$ =58)

c. In 4's: accent every 4th *LH* note (♩ = 58)

d. Also practice the patterns accenting every 6 notes, and finally, every 8 notes.

(The value of accent practice is that it ensures that each individual finger gets equal drill. It is suggested that when practicing in "accents" the student not lift up the accented finger prior to playing it but rather, always begin on the key.)

3. Practice the *LH* in dotted rhythm patterns (as shown below) at ♩ = 88.

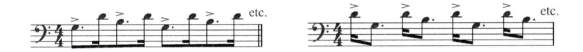

Preparation for octave playing

Since most young students have relatively small hands, they should not be assigned music which requires playing consecutive blocked octaves for an extended period of time. (Although definitely *not* an early level piece, the *LH* in Schumann's "Important Event" is illustrative of such a piece.)

An ideal way for younger students to prepare for octave playing is to start out with consecutive blocked 6ths such as occur in the "Minuet" by Bartok (found in *Keyboard Literature, Book 4,* of *The Music Tree*; Alfred Publ. Co.; used with permission.)

Minuet
from *The First Term at the Piano*

Béla Bartók
(1881-1945)

Andante

If I were assigning this piece, I would ask the student to take several measures and, before playing the blocked 6ths as written, warm up with the exercises shown below.

PRACTICE TIPS

1. *RH* alone, play only finger 5.

2. *RH* alone, play only the thumb.

3. Play the blocked *RH* 6ths broken:

Bottom to top

Top to bottom

(*In future study, this same procedure will be applied to octave scales and also in pieces.*)
When practicing hands separately, I ask students to watch their hands to be sure that there is no excess motion — that they are staying close to the keys and moving laterally without a "pumping" wrist or lifting the fingers off the keys before depressing them.

Practicing octaves

When a student is physically ready to play octaves, it is helpful to start with the playing of *broken* rather than blocked octaves. The Leopold Mozart "Burleske" is an example of a piece which contains a *LH* made entirely of broken octaves. (It also appears in *Keyboard Literature, Book 4,* of *The Music Tree.*)

Burleske
from the Notebook for Wolfgang (1762)

Leopold Mozart
(1719-1787)

A prime consideration when practicing octaves is to avoid the build-up of excessive tension in the playing mechanism. One "trick," of course, is to keep the hand *small* as much as possible. If I were assigning the "Burleske" to a student, I would suggest beginning with the practice tips below.

PRACTICE TIPS

1. In mm. 1-4, play just the *LH* 5th-finger. (*After playing each staccato note, always stop with finger 5 prepared to play the next 5th-finger note.*)

2. Do the same thing with the *LH* thumb notes. (*Be sure that the thumb is always loose and flexible.*)

3. Play both fingers 5 and 1. As you play finger 5, stop prepared for the thumb note; as you play the thumb, stop prepared for the next 5th-finger note, etc. (*Play lightly. Do not stretch open the hand always keep it small, and check to be sure that your wrist and thumb remain loose and flexible.*)

IMPULSE PRACTICE

1. Play the first three *LH* notes (2 + 1) stopping on the third note (finger 5 on the low C#) and with the thumb prepared on the fourth note. A reminder – *keep the hand small.*

2. Play impulses of 4+1. Always begin and end on finger 5 and stop with the thumb pre-
    pared for the next note. (Also play impulses of 6+1 and 8+1.)

3. Do the same impulses (4+1, 6 + 1, and 8+ 1) but this time, always begin and end on
    the thumb, and stop with finger 5 prepared for the next note.

I think that the most important technical point to make about the octaves in the "Burleske" is that
since the *LH* octave skips are to be played detached, the hand never needs to be outstretched to the
size of an octave. It should move back and forth laterally from finger 5 to 1, and at all times remain
small and flexible.

(*To physically experience the hand's flexibility, I often ask students to drop both arms to their sides
and shake out the hands, wrists, and fingers. Then re-position the hands on the keyboard so that the
five fingers are resting on 5 consecutive white keys. This is the normal size of the "natural" hand of
most young students, and this is the hand size that the LH should retain as much as possible when it
plays broken octaves such as those in the "Burleske.")*

The above procedures (playing thumb and fifth fingers alone, playing as broken octaves, and
impulse practice) are also effective when practicing *blocked* octaves. Since the accumulation of
tension is more apt to occur when playing solid octaves, I frequently suggest that when doing
impulse practice, students drop the arms to their sides after each impulse and as suggested above,
shake out the hands, wrists, and fingers. They should also check for free elbows and relaxed shoulders, making sure that the latter are not rigid and elevated.

Developing awareness and control of tension and relaxation in the playing mechanism

It's important to remember that in order to be able to successfully evaluate and maintain the balance of tension (created by muscular contraction) and relaxation, one needs to be physically aware of how both conditions feel. (How does tension *feel*? How does relaxation *feel*?)

To assist students with developing an awareness of this, I frequently have them do stand-up exercises away from the piano which focus on experiencing tension and relaxation in various parts of the body — in the lips, the chin, the jaws, the neck, the shoulders, the arms, the elbows, the wrists, etc. They also need to know how to switch from one condition (tension) to the other (relaxation) on demand. For one example, in a standing position, I ask them to elevate their shoulders and hold them rigidly suspended in that upward position, being aware of the muscular contraction (tension) that is required to do so. Then by abruptly dropping the shoulders back down to their normal position, the student can experience awareness of the relaxation that results from the release of the tension. (Other "body warm-up" exercises are described in Part II of this chapter.)

Practicing phrasing

Although when we think of phrasing we usually do so from the standpoint of musicality, still, when students must deal with shaping phrases, particularly phrase endings, they not only need to know how they should sound but also what to do technically to produce the desired sound.

"Springtime in the Alps," a lovely expressive student/teacher duet by Jon George, from *The Music Tree, Part 2A* (Alfred Publ. Co; used with permission), provides an excellent opportunity to work on artistic phrasing.

In the initial analysis of this piece, the student would observe that it consists of four long phrases, each of which ends on the first beat of a measure, and that the 2nd, 3rd, and 4th phrases each start on a third count upbeat. I use the following practice tips to help the student focus on the shaping of phrase endings.

Springtime in the Alps

Pleasantly

Jon George

PRACTICE TIPS: "BACKWARDS" PRACTICE

1. Begin with the third beat of measure 3 (the *RH A*). Play the *A* and stop on the *LH F#* in measure 4, listening for a tapered ending.

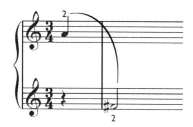

2. Play *all* of measure 3 plus a tapered *F#* over the barline.

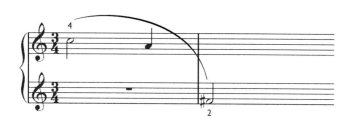

3. In measure 2, begin on the eighth notes on beat 3 and play through the *F#*.

4. Play the whole phrase, listening for a gently tapered *F#* at the end.

By working "backwards," the student's thoughts and ear are programmed to focus on the treatment of the final note of a phrase — how it should sound and what to do technically to produce it.

I do not believe that artistic phrasing is something that only the gifted "superstar" students can do. I think that any student who can hear the difference between a "bump" at the end of a phrase vs. an artistically tapered phrase ending can learn to produce it. Of course the teacher would have to illustrate the desired sound at the lesson and show the student how to practice in order to produce it. The little bit of time it would take to do the four practice tips above is certainly well worth it.

Practicing ornaments

Many years ago, I learned that there are two topics of discussion that should probably be avoided (even among friends) — *religion and politics.* Among musicians, particularly pianists, there's one other subject that probably ought to be added to this "avoid-bringing-it-up-if-at-all-possible" list and that is *how to "properly" execute ornaments!*

In this book I have no intention of addressing the "how-to-execute-ornaments" subject. For those wishing to pursue this issue in a comprehensive, definitive and scholarly manner, I highly recommend a fine book by Walter Emory entitled *Bach's Ornaments.* (First published in 1953 by Novello & Co. LTD, London, it has been reprinted numerous times.) I was won over to this book almost immediately when, on page 10 of its Introduction, the author wrote:

"...there are no absolutely right schemes of ornamentation; but many schemes, each valid in certain circumstances. The player should put aside all ideas of absolute rightness, and aim instead at an attainable goal - a consistent personal style of ornamentation that will serve, like his phrasing and tempi, to distinguish his Bach-playing from other people's."

The balance of the book presents 291 illustrations of Baroque ornaments and proceeds to provide answers for just about everything we might want to know about them but have always been too afraid — or possibly too embarrassed — to ask.

My approach to the subject of ornaments in this segment of *The Success Factor in Piano Teaching* is not on how to *play* them but rather, on how to *practice* them. It seems that all too often, student performances of music containing mordents, trills, turns, appoggiaturas, etc., leave quite a bit to be desired. What might otherwise have turned out to be very commendable performances are frequently marred by stumbles, hesitations, rhythmic errors, and technical glitches whenever an embellishment is encountered. My contention is that when this happens, it's usually because the student either does not understand how the ornament is supposed to sound, or did not know how to deal with it in practice. As examples of the latter, I am using the ornaments in Bach's *Two Part Invention No. 1 in C Major.* (This edition of the Invention appears in the *Festival Collection, Book 6,* edited by Helen Marlais. Published by FJH Music Publishers; used with permission.)

INVENTION No. 1

(BWV 772)

Johann Sebastian Bach
(1685-1750)

Below are the suggestions I would give a student for how to practice the ornaments. (*As with all the practice tips in this book, I suggest to the reader that the best way to understand the practice tips for ornamentation in the Bach Invention is to study this section at the piano, "trying out" each suggested step.*)

For the first week of practice on this Invention, I almost always assign students to practice it hands separately only at a very slow tempo, and *without* the inclusion of any of the ornaments. However, I *would* give the student some exercises for practicing the ornaments outside of the context of the piece.

PRACTICE TIPS FOR WEEK 1

1. *RH* trills (mm. 1, 2, 6, 12, 14, 20): Play each trill starting on *C*, on *D*, on *E*, etc., proceeding upward on white keys, ending on the *C* one octave higher.

2. *RH* trill in m. 8: With fingers 3 and 2, start on *G*, on *A*, *B*, *D* and *E*. Begin with finger 3; finger 2 always playing the black key one half-step lower.

3. *RH* mordent in m. 5, *LH* in m. 13: Play each mordent starting on *C*, *D*, *E*, etc., ending on the *C* one octave higher.

PRACTICE TIPS FOR WEEK 2

Play each different trill or mordent alone as written. Then repeat it but add the one single note of the other hand that plays with the first tone of the embellishment.

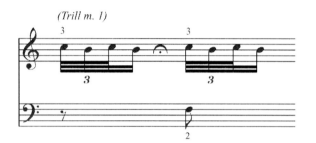

PRACTICE TIPS FOR WEEK 3

1. Embellishment hand only: Approach the embellishment by playing the entire beat that precedes it plus the embellishment.

2. Embellishment hand only: Begin on the embellishment, play through it, and end on the first note of the next beat.

3. Embellishment hand only: Combine steps one and two, *i.e.*, approach the ornament, play the ornament, and play through the beat that follows it.

4. Same as step 3, but add the other hand.

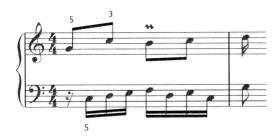

PRACTICE TIPS FOR WEEK 4

1. Ornament hand only: Play the whole measure containing the ornament, stopping on the first note of the next measure.

2. *HT*: Same as step one but add the other hand.

Of course during the four weeks described above, the student would also have been practicing the Invention *without* adding the ornaments. By week 5, he should be able to play it *HT,* and securely at a moderate tempo. Assuming that as preparation, the student has done ornament exercises such as those illustrated above, adding them now to the piece should be relatively easy provided that he selects a wise "thinking" tempo.

Needless to say, it would not be possible (or even desirable) to write out all of these practice steps during the lesson. *What's important is that each step is illustrated by the teacher and then successfully executed by the student.* While this is actually occurring, we can talk through the practice steps and illustrate each of them on the student's audio or video recording device so that he can have a daily model for exactly how to work at home.

In workshops, I am often asked, *"Do you really do all of these practice steps with your students when they are studying this Invention or other works which contain similar ornamentation?"*

My answer is always *"Absolutely! And I can, in all honesty, say that I cannot remember ever having a student who had difficulty executing ornaments if he or she were technically ready to deal with them and had a way to practice them!"*

"Backwards" practice

When playing extended "runs," students frequently bog down as they approach the end of the passage, and at this point, the "run" seems to "self-destruct." An example of such a passage occurs in the first two lines of the "Gigue" by Arnold. (This is found in *Keyboard Literature, Part 3,* of *The Music Tree;* Dist. By Alfred Publ. Co. Used with permission.)

Gigue
From *Lessons for Harpsichord*

Samuel Arnold
(1740-1802)

Below are suggested practice steps for the *RH* run in mm. 1-4 to ensure that the end of this passage is as secure and well-controlled as the beginning.

PRACTICE TIPS

1. In m. 4, play the last three notes of the run plus the first note of the next measure. Be sure to start on the correct finger.

2. In m. 4, play the last six notes of the run plus the first note of the next measure.

3. Continue working backwards, always adding three additional notes to the run.

then

Continue adding three notes to the beginning of the run in this manner until the entire phrase is complete.

In summary, in order for ends of runs to be as secure and well-controlled as beginnings, students must spend as much practice time starting at the end of the run and working backwards as they do starting at its beginning.

(And the same thing is true for pieces! Students who always start their practice at the beginning of a piece usually end up with secure openings and weak endings. In practice, there must always be a rotation of sections, i.e., one day start at the beginning; the following day play the last section first; on day three start with the middle section, etc.)

Practicing "basic" pedaling in early-level pieces

I classify pedaling as one of the components of piano technique. I also believe that the proper execution of pedaling and pedal practice are both important parts of the "mechanics" which must be dealt with prior to being able to successfully focus on musicality. Thinking back on my own student days, I don't recall actually being assigned pedal practice until late in my teenage years. I believe that Isabelle Vengerova was the first teacher to really make the point of the importance of such practice with me, and I vividly recall this happening as we worked together on Chopin's *Ballade No. 4 in F Minor.*

Because I was seemingly so unaware of what my foot was doing in this piece, Mme. V. assigned pedal practice which, for every pedal change, involved the actual lifting of my right foot off of the pedal and raising my entire leg about a dozen inches up off of the floor! As you can imagine, this (horrific!) remedial approach to using the pedal very soon awakened me to the importance of needing to know as much about what my foot was doing both on and off the pedal as I did about the rest of my playing mechanism!

Over the many years since my "Vengerova Experience" with the pedal, as I listen to students perform in recitals, contests, and auditions, I continue to find artistic use of the pedal as one of the things that needs the most attention — even in the performances of those students who might otherwise be classified as "gifted." I believe that artistic and properly executed pedaling is something that all students can learn to do and do well regardless of their innate musical "talent." But as with everything else, this will only happen if the teacher effectively deals with it the very first time a student is assigned a piece which requires the use of the pedal, and continues to follow-up on it until it becomes a part of the student's habit.

In my studio, before ever considering the addition of pedal to a piece of music, my students know that they must first be able to prove that they are able to play the piece 100% accurately without it. When it's time to add the pedal, the first step is always to plan and mark it onto the score unless the composer or editor has already done so.

One of my own compositions, "Gentle Breeze" from *Solo Flight* (Alfred Publ. Co. Used with permission), provides an opportunity for early-level students to learn how to properly execute simple basic pedaling before having to deal with more refined syncopated pedaling.

As soon as the student can play "Gentle Breeze" accurately, then she is ready to add the pedal. Before doing so, she'll observe that there are four long pedals in it — that in lines 1, 2, and 3, the pedal goes down on beat one and lifts on the quarter rest (beat 6) at the end of the line. In the fourth line it remains down through the entire last measure.

Gentle Breeze

PRACTICE TIPS

1. Depress the pedal and play only mm. 4 and 8, slowly, counting. On count six (the quarter rest), say "up" instead of "six" as you lift the pedal.

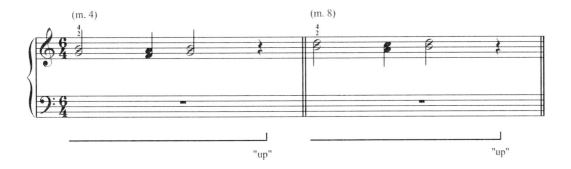

2. Play mm. 4 and 5, slowly, counting. Say "up" on count 6, and in m. 5, say "down" on the first beat.

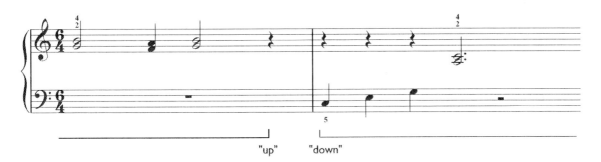

> (I have found that verbalizing the action of the foot on the pedal by using words such as "up," "hold," and "down" is very helpful to students in their initial experiences of practicing pedaling.)

3. Play whole piece, counting and continuing to verbalize the action of the foot as suggested in step 2 above.

In my opinion, students need to have considerable success executing basic pedaling in early-level pieces such as "Gentle Breeze" before being assigned music that requires syncopated pedaling.

Presenting syncopated pedaling

When I introduce *syncopated* pedaling, I always do so in a simple exercise instead of in a piece of music. The exercise consists of a one-octave C major scale to be played *HT* using only the 3rd fingers of each hand.

SYNCOPATED PEDAL EXERCISE

The student is asked to always overlap two scale tones with the pedal held down before changing it so that the resulting blur is obvious.

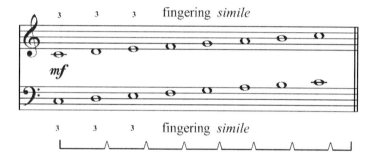

(I think it's very important for students to actually hear the blur that results from this two-tone overlap so that they become aurally aware of the difference in sound between clarity and blur. I am convinced that many times, when students' playing lacks clarity when executing pedal changes, they themselves really don't hear it. A good point to make with students as we work with them on pedaling is that it's actually the ear rather than the foot which must control the use of the pedal.)

Practicing syncopated pedaling within pieces

Once students are able to coordinate syncopated pedaling in an activity such as the C Major scale exercise shown above, they are ready to be assigned pieces which require such pedaling. If the pedaling cues in the music have not been indicated by the composer or editor, or if the performer wants to modify given pedaling in some way, then these changes must first be planned and marked onto the score before it can be practiced.

"Falling Leaves," a lovely, expressive piece by David Kraehenbuehl, provides an excellent opportunity for practicing syncopated pedaling. (This piece is in *Students' Choice, Part 4*, of *The Music Tree*; Dist. by Alfred Publ. Co. Used with permission.) Although the printed pedal indications that appear in the excerpt of "Falling Leaves" shown below are fairly standard for most printed piano music, they actually do not accurately depict what the foot must do to ensure 100% clarity whenever the pedal changes occur.

Falling Leaves

Slowly and freely

David Kraehenbuehl

In the "edited" copy below, I have written into the score exactly what I think the foot must do in order to achieve the desired clarity whenever the pedal changes.

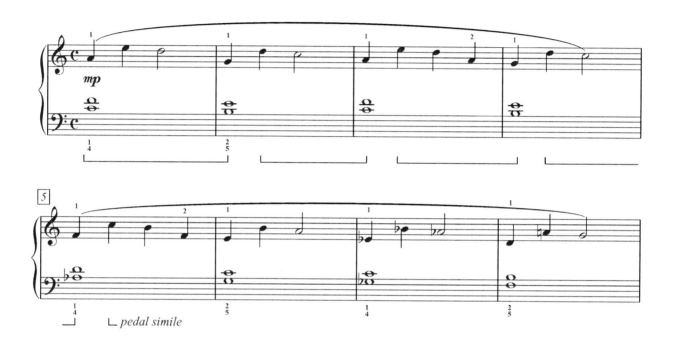

PRACTICE TIPS

1.   At a super slow tempo, play and count *LH* alone, always lifting the pedal on count one and depressing it on count 2 as shown above. *Always pause whenever the pedal lifts in order to listen for clarity.*

2.   Do step one again, but this time play *HT. Continue to pause whenever the pedal lifts.*

3.   At a super slow tempo, play *HT* again but now without pausing. (Once again, many students find it helpful to continue verbalizing what the foot is actually doing as they play.)

The pedaling in "Prayer" by Gurlitt (from *Keyboard Literature Part 4* of *The Music Tree*; Dist. by Alfred Publ. Co. Used with permission.) is a bit more complex than that in "Falling Leaves," simply because a change has to occur twice in nearly every measure.

Prayer

Cornelius Gurlitt
(1820-1901)

The edited example below illustrates my suggestions for pedaling in the "Prayer."

PRACTICE TIPS

1. Practicing in 4-measure segments at a very slow tempo (♩ = 60), play *LH* alone, counting "1-2-3-4." Lift the pedal on counts 1 and 3, and depress it on counts 2 and 4 as shown above.

    STOP on beats 3 and 1, listening for clarity. (Once again, counting aloud and verbalizing the "ups" and "downs" of the foot will assist the student with executing this syncopated pedaling.)

2. Do step one *HT*. (Continue to pause on beats 1 and 3.)

3. Do step two again but without pauses.

I usually find that when students can do the LH alone with pedal, more often than not, they are able then to successfully coordinate both hands together with pedal.

As soon as the *HT* coordination of syncopated pedaling has been achieved in the first four measures of this one-page piece, students should have no problems with it in the rest of the piece because it is essentially the same throughout.

In summary

In Part I of this chapter, we have been discussing and illustrating how students can become secure with the technical demands of their pieces by creating exercises out of challenging structural elements contained in them and practicing these along with working on the piece itself. As indicated throughout, I often encourage my students to use such exercises as daily "warm-ups" before they actually begin to practice the piece *per se.*

Although I think that using the above approach to technical practice is a *must,* I also think that, in addition, students can enhance their basic technical skills by practicing exercises *apart from* their pieces — things such as 5-finger patterns, scales, arpeggios, chords, Hanon studies, octaves, trills, chromatics, legato 3rds, etc. Thus, Part II of this chapter focuses on this latter approach to teaching and practicing technique.

▶ PART II: DEVELOPING TECHNICAL SKILLS VIA EXERCISES APART FROM PIECES

Introduction

The upside of practicing technique via exercises apart from pieces of music is that *reading does not have to be involved.* I am very opposed to students *reading* technique exercises out of a book — from a scale or arpeggio book, from a Hanon collection, etc., because, when their eyes are glued to the music, they are unable to focus all of their attention onto the look and feel of the playing mechanism and the sounds being produced. When practicing technique exercises, I want students, as much as possible, to be sensitive to how their body *feels* when they are playing, i.e., maintaining loose, flexible wrists and elbows, tension-free shoulders, etc. I also want them to be aware of the *look* of the hand — the condition of the arch, the positioning of the fingers on the keys, etc. Equally important, they need to be keenly aware of the *sounds* they are producing. I maintain that *reading* exercises substantially limits a student's ability to remain 100% focused on the physical, visual, and aural aspects of technical practice.

The downside of practicing technique via exercises apart from pieces is a tendency to become disengaged and robotic. Here's a stunning example of this: Beginning in junior high school, I always started every practice period by doing my technique routines — scales, arpeggios, trills, octaves, chords, etc. I remember that during this segment of my practice, over a period of time I actually read all of *Gone with the Wind*, as well as numerous Nancy Drew mysteries and other books, plus every *Superman* and *Batman* comic book I could get my hands on. Perhaps you're wondering how my parents (*neither of whom could read or play a note of music*) reacted to this. Well, since the piano was in the living room and the door to that room was always closed when I was working there, my parents never entered it during my practice. To this day, I am sure that they (*bless their souls*) never knew what was actually going on in there because all of that flashy technical practice probably sounded pretty impressive to them!

Technique exercises and goals

In *The Success Factor in Piano Teaching* I make no attempt to provide a comprehensive presentation of all of the exercises that I assign to my students. Nor do I intend to advocate or delve into the physical approaches of any specific "schools" of piano playing. Rather, the plan here is simply to highlight some of the basic considerations for the development of technique which I think should form the core of every well-structured curriculum, and to present illustrations of a few of the exercises that I have found useful over the years, both as a pianist and a teacher.

Because of the personal experience described above, as a teacher I always try to make sure that whenever my students are assigned technique exercises, they are also assigned *specific* things to think about and/or to look and listen for. Here are a few examples:

- "When playing the *RH* of your ascending scale, watch your thumb and check to be sure that it remains flexible as it slides under your hand for the crossings."

- "Listen to be sure that your thumbs do not produce accents when they pass under your hand."

- "In your Hanon study, watch fingers 2-3-4 of your *LH* to be sure that they are playing up on their 'pads' rather than being extended out straight."

- "When you are playing arpeggios, watch your wrists to be sure that they are not dipping downward every time your thumb goes under."

- "When practicing your scales, listen for a full, rich *legato* sound, and make sure that all tones are equally matched in volume."

Physical sensitivity

As I see it, one of the most important goals when teaching technique is to help students develop a sensitivity to the *body's* relationship to the keyboard — an acute physical awareness of the *whole* mechanism from the head down and from the feet up. To help early level students begin to acquire this awareness, I start with what we call "body warm-ups" to be done away from the piano. For these "loosening up" exercises, which we usually do at the beginning of the lesson, I ask students to stand and focus on individual components of the body as described below.

BODY WARM-UP EXERCISES (to be done standing up away from the piano)

1. *The head:* Lower and raise the chin and head; check for relaxed lips and jaw with no clenched teeth, etc.

2. *Shoulder lifts:* Begin with the shoulders in a dropped-down, comfortable position free of all muscular contraction (tension); then, contracting the muscles, elevate the shoulders and hold them in a rigid, pulled-up position (to experience the resulting tension). End by allowing the shoulders to drop back down and settle into their natural, relaxed, hanging-down position.

3. *Arm swings:* Begin with both arms hanging loosely at the sides; then vigorously swing both of them simultaneously, forward and backward. Also, taking one arm at a time, let it swing freely from side to side in front of the body.

4. *Elbow lifts:* Begin with the arms hanging loosely at the sides. Gradually lift the two arms to waist level by outward lifts of the elbows; hold the arms in that position for a moment and then release the contraction and let both arms flop back down to the sides.

5. *Wrist flaps:* Raise one arm at a time and with a loose, flexible wrist, wave "bye-bye."

6. *Hand and finger "shake-outs":* With arms hanging loosely down at the sides, vigorously shake out the hands and fingers.

I do these body warm-ups with my beginners, starting at their very first lesson. It's a great way to begin a lesson and the students seem to enjoy doing them. I have also found such exercises to be extremely useful for intermediate and advanced students — especially those who exhibit an excess of accumulated tension in various parts of the body when they play, but are either unaware of it or don't know what to do to control it.

Over the years, I have become increasingly convinced that students who experience and can, on demand, create and control muscular activities such as those above *away from the piano,* are usually able to transfer them to many of the sensations and physical activities which occur when they are playing the piano. Although we never spend more than two or three minutes of lesson time on them, in my opinion, the resulting conscious sensitivity to the body is well worth the time spent.

Posture at the piano

I believe that once students are seated at the piano, all subsequent technical habits grow out of the quality of their posture. Here again, students must develop sensitivity to where and how they sit at the instrument. This entails an awareness of:

- *Sitting at the correct height and distance from the keys.* Students must *know* if they are sitting too high or too low, too close or too far back from the keys and adjust the bench as needed.

- *Sitting "tall" — no slumping!* If a student is slumping, it's a good idea to check the height of the bench because sometimes slumping results from a bench that is too high. Once the correct height is determined, I think it's a good idea to measure the distance from the floor up to the seat and then ask students (or a parent) to make this same measurement at home.

- *Sitting on the edge of the bench* (or chair) with the body weight evenly distributed between the feet and seat. By "edge" of the bench, I am referring to the front third of the bench's surface that is closest to the keyboard. This sitting position allows the student to feel the freedom of moving both forward and backward, and from side to side. It is the opposite of being "bench-bound" — a more static condition that results from sitting further back on the bench with the *derriere* covering most of the bench's surface.

- *Sitting with both feet flat on the floor* unless using the pedal. In the case of young children whose legs are too short to reach the floor, they must either sit further back on the bench with their ankles crossed, or use some sort of a platform for their feet. Above all, *no dangling legs* because this impairs both rhythmic stability and body balance.

If we want to develop students who are truly conscious of their body's relationship to the keyboard, then at every lesson and before every piece, we need to have them perform the ritual of checking on all of the above things — the height of the bench and its distance from the keyboard, the positioning of the feet, the posture, and the sitting position on the bench. If we consistently have students go through this checklist every time they sit down at the piano, sooner or later correct physical posture at the instrument will indeed become part of their habit and we can finally put this matter on "cruise control." *O happy day!* (As an aside, I believe that it's very important for parents to be aware of the things that constitute correct posture at the instrument. This is something I always discuss and illustrate in detail for the parents of all new students. It's also the kind of thing that one might even take a couple of minutes to discuss and illustrate at a piano program, assuming that the format of the program is informal.)

Technical goals and exercises for beginners

The following list represents most of the basic technical skills I expect my beginners to acquire during their first year of study. By the end of approximately nine months of lessons, they should be able to:

- play fingers 2-3 and 2-3-4 *legato* on groups of two and three black keys. *This is where the sound and the "feel" of artistic phrasing actually begins.*

- play fingers 1 and 5 as a blocked 5th on white keys. *This helps "size" and shape the hand for a five-finger position and also strengthens the outside structure of the hand which supports the arch.*

- play fingers 2-3 and 2-3-4 both *legato* and *staccato* on consecutive white keys.

- play fingers 1-2-3-4-5 both *legato* and *staccato* on five consecutive white keys.

- play blocked fifths changing to blocked 6ths by either moving the thumb away from the hand or by moving fingers 2-3-4-5 out away from the thumb.

- play major and minor 5-finger patterns in the keys of *C, G, D, A, E,* and *F,* both hands separately *(HS)* and hands together *(HT),* both *legato* and *staccato,* and both parallel and contrary motion.

- play major and minor 5-finger patterns with one hand playing *legato* vs. the other hand playing *staccato.*

- play fingers 1-3-5 of major and minor triads in the above keys going up and down, broken, and ending with a blocked triad. (Example for *RH:* Fingers 1-3-5, 5-3-1, 1-3-5-3-1, plus a blocked triad.)

My students practice major and minor five-finger patterns via the playing of short, easy-to-remember "rote" patterns such as these:

Pattern 1

Pattern 2

Pattern 3

Patterns such as the these are presented by rote at the lesson and never require reading. Thus, students are at all times free to observe and evaluate their hand and finger positions as well as the quantity and quality of the sound they are producing.

Scales

At some point near the end of their first year of study, students should be ready to begin scale-playing. The technical studies they have practiced thus far have helped to develop finger independence, tonal projection, evenness and clarity, and facility within a five-finger position.

Before beginning scales, students need to be proficient with two skills:

1. playing fingers 1-2-3, 1-2-3-4, and 1-2-3-4-5 clearly, evenly, and *legato* within a five-finger position, and

2. executing *legato* connections between two five-finger patterns by either sliding the thumb under the hand or passing the hand over and across the thumb (scale "crossings").

PREPARATION OF THE THUMB FOR SCALE CROSSINGS

As preparation for playing scales, students must first practice exercises that focus on just the movement of the thumb. The following exercises illustrate some of the preparatory "crossing" exercises I assign. (*In such exercises, I emphasize that the thumb must slide under the hand via the second joint and must remain flexible.*)

Exercise 1 - Silently depress finger 2 and hold while playing the thumb *pp*.

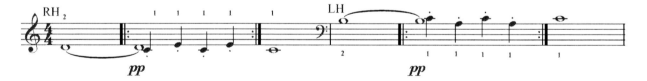

Exercise 1a - Silently depress fingers 2 and 3 and hold while playing the thumb.

Exercise 2 – Play on every white key from *C* to *C*. (*RH is shown; LH plays the same but in reverse.*)

and

and

The presentation of scales

As soon as students can successfully execute the previous thumb motion exercises, they should be ready to begin scale-playing *per se*. The first scale I assign is *D*-flat Major — one of the three that are the easiest. (*B* Major and *F#* Major are equally good as starters.) The keyboard topography of these three scales (five black keys and two white keys) makes it easy for students to understand and remember the fingering because it's so logical. Of course one would use the three longest fingers (2, 3 and 4) on the black keys because they are the furthest away, and the short finger (the thumb) is the logical choice for the two white keys. (As an interesting aside, it is recorded that because of the above reasons, the scale of *B* Major was always the one which Chopin chose to assign first to his students.)

PREPARATORY EXERCISES FOR SCALE PLAYING

Blocked

Students need to know that every scale consists of just *two* finger positions — a "1-2-3" and a "1-2-3-4" position. The first practice step I assign with each new scale is to block these two groups *HS*, up and down the keyboard as shown below in the next example. This really helps to reinforce both the topography and the fingering of the scale.

"Skeleton" Scales

Playing *only* fingers 1-3 and 1-4 in "skeleton" scales provides an excellent way to focus on the action of the thumb and the positioning of fingers 3 and 4 within the scale.

Playing the complete scale

After practicing preparatory exercises such as those previously illustrated, the student should then be ready to play the whole scale up and down, two octaves, beginning and ending on the keynote, *D*-flat. Over the next two weeks students use the following practice plans.

SCALE PRACTICE PLAN 1

1. For the first week, I assign the scale to be played *HS* only, up and down two octaves at ♩ = 60 (playing one tone with every metronome tick).

    (*I think it's important that right from the beginning, every scale is always played at least two octaves because, otherwise, the student does not have the experience of playing crossings which involve both fingers 3 and 4.*)

2. When secure *HS*, the student is ready to play the scale *HT* in parallel motion. Here again, the D-flat, F♯, and B Major scales are the easiest to coordinate *HT* because the two thumbs always play at the same time, and fingers 2-3 and 2-3-4 always mirror each other on the groups of two and three black keys.

SCALE PRACTICE PLAN 2

1. *HT*: first block fingers 2-3 and 2-3-4 and connect the two blocks with the thumbs as shown.

2. When the above exercise is easy, play the complete scale parallel motion, *HT*, up and down two octaves, beginning and ending on the keynote, D-flat at ♩ = 60 (with one tone per tick).

The steps suggested above for the preparation and practice of the *D-flat Major* scale comprise the procedure I use for the presentation and assignment of *all* scales. By the time my students who began lessons at age seven or eight reach high school, I expect them to be able to play all of the major and harmonic minor scales, *HT*, four octaves at ♩ = 60 (playing four tones per tick.) My most advanced (and serious) students often go on to achieve the ability to play six and sometimes even eight notes per tick, and many of them also practice the natural and melodic minor scales as well as the harmonic form.

Variations for scale practice

Without a doubt, scale practice often becomes a turn-off for many students. I believe that one reason this happens is because they always practice them the same way — usually up and down, maybe just two octaves (or sometimes three or four octaves), but still, always *up and down*.

In order to maintain interest in playing scales, students need to have variety in their practice routines. For one example, why not assign scales to be practiced *down and up* as opposed to always playing them up and down? In music they certainly occur in both formats so why not practice them both ways? — maybe one week, do *down and up* first, and then the following week, *up and down*. Just a minor change such as this can often provide relief from the boredom that can occur when one always does just the same old "six and seven," day after day and week after week.

Below are a number of other suggested routines which can add variety to scale-practice.

SCALE PRACTICE ROUTINE 1

HT, nonstop, play up two octaves in *parallel* motion, then out and back in, two octaves in *contrary* motion, then continue on up two more octaves in *parallel* motion and end by playing the complete scale down, four octaves, in *parallel* motion.

SCALE PRACTICE ROUTINE 2

Both *HS* and *HT*, practice in "accents" (suggested practice tempo: ♩ = 60.)

(On the accented notes, always begin the accented finger on the key and do a swift downward thrust of the finger; keep a firm nail joint; do not lift a finger up off of a key either before or after depressing it; check to be sure that the wrist always remains loose and flexible after each accented tone.)

a. Play up and down, two octaves, in "accents" of 1's: (play one note per tick, accenting every tone.)
b. Play up and down, two octaves, in "accents" of 2's: (play two tones per tick, accenting every other tone.)
c. Play up and down, three octaves, in "accents" of 3's: (play three tones per tick, accenting every 3rd tone.)
d. Play up and down, four octaves, in "accents" of 4's: (play four tones per tick, accenting every 4th tone.)
    (More advanced students can also practice scales in accents of 6's and 8's.)

As previously stated, practicing in "accents" ensures that each finger receives individual attention and guarantees both evenness and clarity in articulation.

SCALE PRACTICE ROUTINE 3

HS only, play two octaves up and down, beginning and ending on each scale degree.

> *For example, in the C Major scale:*
> a. play the *RH* up and down two octaves, beginning and ending with the thumb on *C*; then
> b. begin and end with finger 2 on the 2nd scale degree (*D*); then
> c. begin and end with finger 3 on the 3rd scale degree (*E*), etc.
> d. do the same procedure for the *LH*.

SCALE PRACTICE ROUTINE 4

Begin low on the keyboard. *HT*: up and down <u>two</u> octaves, play <u>two</u> scale tones in the *RH* for every one tone in the *LH*.

Repeat the scale, but this time play up and down <u>three</u> octaves with <u>three</u> notes in the *RH* and only one in the *LH*.

Finally, play up and down <u>four</u> octaves with <u>four</u> notes in the *RH* for every one note in the *LH*.

For LH practice do the opposite:
Begin *high* on the keyboard and play down and then up. Do the same process shown above, but now the *LH* is the "traveling" hand, playing two, three, and finally four notes for every one *RH* note.

SCALE PRACTICE ROUTINE 5

Two against three: Begin *low* on the keyboard. With the hands two octaves apart, play duplets in the *LH* and triplets in the *RH*. (The *RH* will complete three octaves while the *LH* only plays two.)

Repeat this exercise, but begin *high* on the keyboard, playing duplets in the *RH* and triplets with the *LH*.

SCALE PRACTICE ROUTINE 6

Play scales in 6ths.

Play scales in 10ths.

Play scales in 3rds.

SCALE PRACTICE ROUTINE 7

Play scales using a variety of touches.

For example:
   a. play both hands *staccato*;
   b. play one hand *staccato* and the other hand *legato*, etc.

SCALE PRACTICE ROUTINE 8

Play using different dynamic levels.

For example:
a. play all *f*;
b. play all *p*;
c. play two octaves *f* and the next 2 octaves *p*;
d. play one hand *f* and the other hand *p*;
e. begin *p* and play four octaves, adding a *crescendo*;
f. begin *f* and play four octaves, adding a *diminuendo*.

SCALE PRACTICE ROUTINE 9

Bi-tonal scales:

a. play one hand in a major (or minor) key and the other hand in its parallel minor (or major) key;
b. play one hand in a major (or minor) key and the other hand in a different major (or minor) key.

Obviously because there are so many different ways to practice scales, no student should ever have a reason to become bored.

Arpeggios, octaves, chords, trills, legato 3rds, chromatics, etc.

Beginning in about the third year of lessons, along with scales, my students' technique routines usually begin to include exercises dealing with other things such as chromatics, arpeggios, octaves, chords (major, minor, augmented and diminished 7ths), legato 3rds, trills, etc. What is assigned depends upon the size of the students' hands and their individual needs based on the repertoire they are playing. Although no exercises for developing technical skills other than scales are being included in this book, suffice it to say that, as with scales, there are also multiple ways to assign and practice each of these other elements.

A final suggestion

As previously stated, I strongly recommend that students do not *read* any technical exercises out of a book for the following three reasons:

1. this practice often impedes the student's understanding and memory of scale fingering;
2. reading diminishes the student's ability to watch and evaluate his hands/fingers as they play; and
3. it limits the ability to focus on the sound that is being produced.

In summary

We know that students who are ill-equipped to deal successfully with the technical challenges they find in their music — especially those who are poor readers — usually do not enjoy continuing study over an extended period of time. Therefore, as teachers, it is our responsibility to provide our students with a comprehensive curriculum designed to produce technical expertise, one that can be successfully implemented in the performance of the repertoire they are assigned.

As we think about the teaching and practicing of technique, it is good to continue reminding ourselves and our students of its purpose — to provide the physical skills necessary for expressing the musical content of the pieces that are assigned. We must be sure that the technique they acquire always produces performances which not only demonstrate a mastery of the keyboard, but also present a *clear differentiation between robotics and music-making!*

From Presentation to Performance — Getting It All Together

In Chapter 7, the focus was on technique and the presentation of practice strategies designed to equip students with a variety of skills needed in order to be able to successfully learn and perform their repertoire with technical ease and security. The subject was approached from the following points of view:

- **creating and practicing exercises derived from elements found in the music itself.** As examples, we isolated various structural elements from elementary and intermediate level repertoire which frequently provide technical challenges for many students, and suggested practice procedures that will assist in dealing with them effectively — *all specific things that students should be doing when they practice instead of just sitting at the piano and resorting to mindless, goal-less repetitions.*

- **practicing exercises apart from a musical context (5-finger drills, scales, arpeggios, etc.)**

In this chapter we are going to take a look at the following three early advanced solos:

> *Fantasie in D Minor, K. 397,* by Mozart
> *Fantasy Dance, Op. 124, No. 5,* by Schumann
> *Notturno, Op. 54, No. 4,* by Grieg

(All three of these pieces appear in numerous collections. For this discussion, I have chosen to use Helen Marlais' edition of these works found in the *Festival Collection* of the "Succeeding with the Masters" series, published by the FJH Music Co. and used with permission. The Schumann *Fantasy Dance* appears in Book 6 of the *Festival Collection*, and the Mozart and Grieg pieces are in Book 7.)

The plan is to examine in detail the content of each piece from the standpoint of both its musical "message," and its formal structure, along with providing tips for teaching and practicing the piece as it evolves from its initial presentation at the lesson through its actual artistic performance.

▶ FANTASIE IN D MINOR, K. 397 BY MOZART

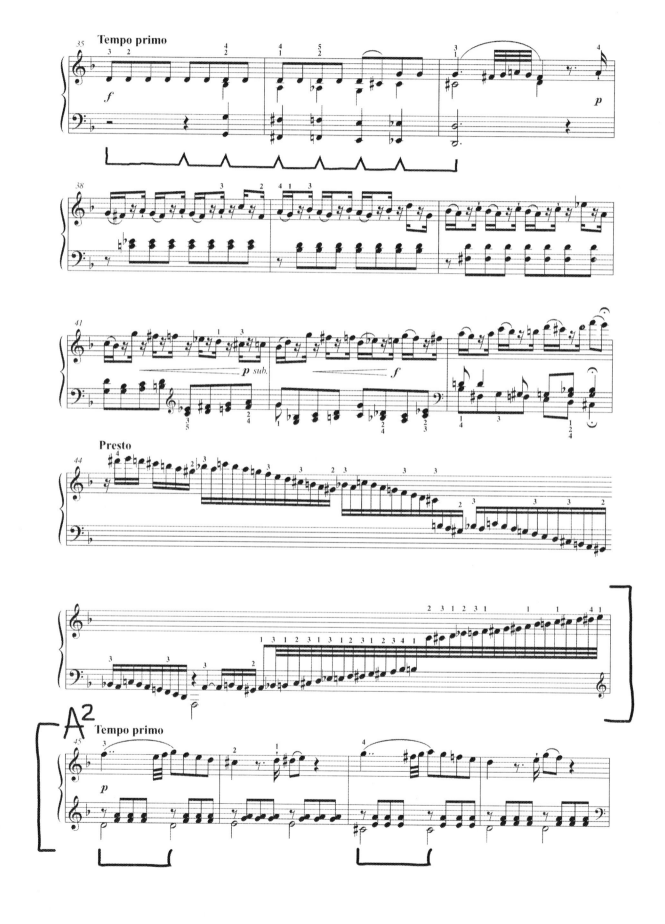

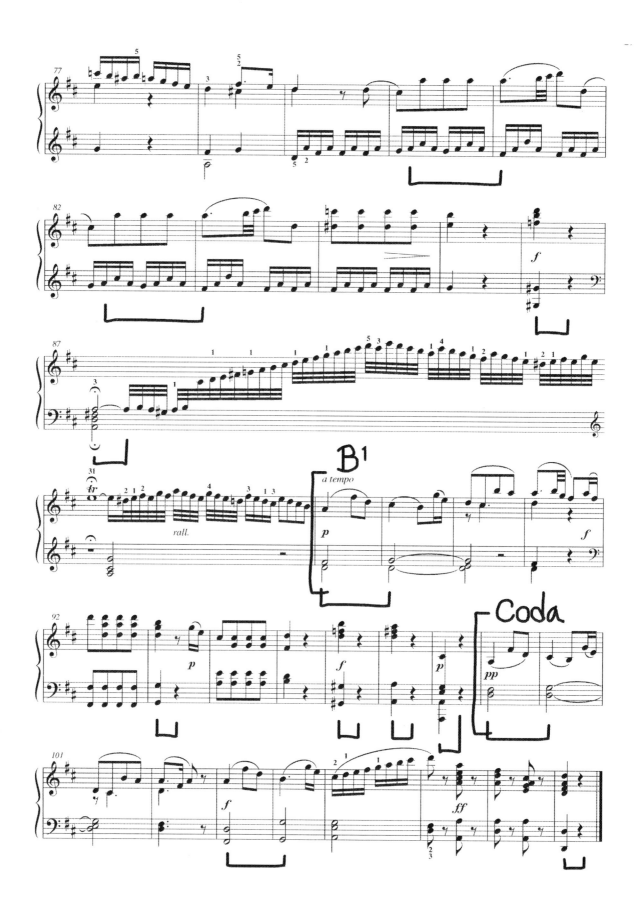

THE INITIAL PRESENTATION AT THE LESSON

Step One: *Discussing what the piece is about*

If music is indeed a communicative art form, then I believe that the first step in the presentation of every new piece should be a discussion of what the piece is about — what ideas and feelings was the composer seeking to convey with the music? Part of the answer to this question lies in the piece's title, *i.e.*, "What is a Nocturne?", a "Gigue?", a "Fugue?", a "Fantasy?", an "Invention?", etc. It seems that all too often when students are asked questions such as these about the music they are playing, they don't have an answer. Since the title of a piece often provides valuable clues for its interpretation, students always need to consider the kind of impact the title might have on the music's performance.

With a piece such as the Mozart *Fantasie*, I usually plan to spend the entire lesson time on its initial presentation. As I see it, the first step would be to discuss the implications of its title — what characteristics might we expect in a Classical Period fantasy? One definition is music that depicts numerous "free flights of fancy." For Mozart, this form provided freedom to depart from the generally accepted rules governing 18th century composition and allowed him to experiment with the formal structure. In his *Fantasie in D Minor*, he has definitely created an improvisatory character brought about by dramatic and often unexpected changes of dynamics, tempo, touch, and mood throughout.

Step Two: *Hearing a performance of the piece* (as preparation for analysis)

After the above discussion, the next important step would be to actually hear the piece. (*How can we expect students to be enthusiastic about learning to play a piece that they've never heard?*) If I were going to assign the Mozart *Fantasie* to a student, perhaps a week before the actual presentation, I would ask him to listen to the excellent CD performance of it that is included along with Book 7 of the *Festival Collection*. Then, at the lesson, I would also play and talk it through. As the student listens, I would ask him to follow the score so that after the performance, he will be ready to analyze the piece's formal structure and mark and label its various parts.

Step Three: *Analyzing the piece's formal structure*

The Introduction (mm. 1-11)
The introduction of the *Fantasie* is somewhat straight forward and somber — even a bit mysterious sounding. It might be likened to the ebb and flow of gentle waves. Perhaps its main purpose is simply to get our attention and make us wonder about what is going to happen once the actual drama begins.

The A section (mm. 12-54)
This part actually features three contrasting musical ideas:

1. The first idea (mm. 12-19) is marked *p* and consists of a simple and somewhat plaintive upper voice melody, plus a lower bass progression (the *LH* down-stem notes) with harmony in the middle. It occurs two more times in the piece — mm. 29-33, and mm. 45-54. In each of these three occurrences, the sudden changes from *p* to *f* are always unexpected surprises!

2. The second idea appears in mm. 20-22 and 35-37. These moments are marked *f*, and are made of descending *LH* bass octaves. When these octaves are coupled with the *RH* part, the resulting 4-note chords create an entirely different character from the opening theme — now much more forceful and dramatic, perhaps even a bit stern.

3. The third idea (mm. 23-27, and 38-43) uses two-note slurs, staccatos, and rests in the upper part, plus the *LH* accompaniment of repeated eighth notes to create a somewhat agitated and unsettled atmosphere.

Throughout the piece, whenever Mozart decides to abruptly abandon one musical idea and move to another, he frequently signals these departures by inserting rests and fermatas (m. 28), and/or *presto* cadenzas (m. 34).

The B section (*Allegretto* — mm. 55 to the end)
In m. 55, the sudden shift from *D* Minor to *D* Major, the *dolce* indication, and the tempo change all create an entirely different character from any that has previously occurred. It suddenly seems like a brand new piece! Now its mood is happy and carefree, like a bright fresh spring day, and it remains so until mm. 85-87, when Mozart presents a brief reminder of what has come before and makes us wonder about what is still to come. But the composer cleverly brings back the B theme in m. 88, and all ends well. (M. 99 to the end might be considered a coda.)

Step Four: *Marking and labeling the parts*

Depending upon who's doing the analysis, there are usually always several ways the various parts might be marked and labeled. The full score shows one possibility.

Step Five: *Creating the first week's assignment*

With most students, I usually do not assign a workout of the whole *Fantasie* for the first week of practice on it. More than likely the assignment would be the Introduction (mm 1-11), the A parts (mm. 12-33, 35-43, and 45-54), and the cadenzas (mm. 34, 44, 53, and 87).

SUGGESTIONS FOR PRACTICE AND PERFORMANCE

I ask my students to always work out their new pieces slowly and using a full, rich tone. Things which affect a piece's musical interpretation — dynamics, tempo changes such as *rit.* and *accel.*, pedaling, etc. — are postponed until the student has achieved accuracy and technical security with the entire piece. Below are a few ideas to consider relative to the musical interpretation of the *Fantasie* along with some suggestions for practice.

Working out the introduction (mm. 1-11)

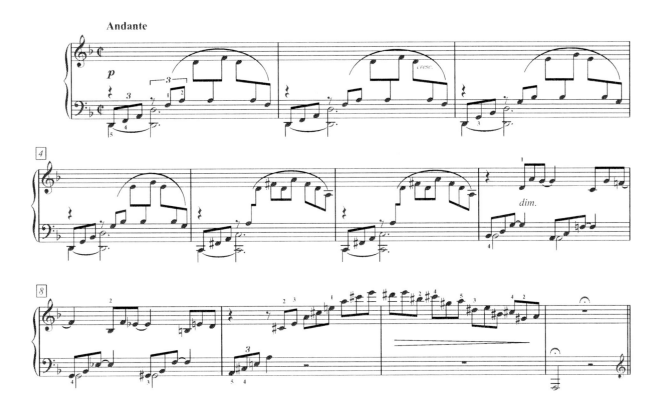

PRACTICE SUGGESTIONS

1. *HS:* Block the chord changes using the "play-prepare" procedure. *This not only helps to physically "program" the technique but also aurally highlights the harmonic progression.*
2. Play both hands *blocked*, using alternate hands, L, R, L, R, etc., and no pedal.
3. Play *HT* as written. *When playing as written, attention should be given to the LH ties and the sustained dotted half-note octaves.*

Performing the introduction

- **Tempo:** Performers should be aware that the tempo marking of the introduction is *Andante* (and not *Adagio*). In addition, the *alla breve* time signature suggests a feeling of *two* beats per measure (as opposed to *four*). Both of these things are significant because they suggest that even though the character of the Introduction is somewhat somber and reserved, Mozart must have wanted the music to convey at least a moderate amount of motion in the up and down wave-like passages.

- **Dynamics:** The performer should avoid adding *cresc.* and/or *dim.* unless indicated in the score.

- **Pedaling:** Some pedaling is acceptable but only if used sparingly. (The full score includes some suggestions for pedaling possibilities throughout the piece.)

Practicing and performing the A section

PRACTICE SUGGESTIONS

Idea One

In working out *idea one* of the A section (mm. 12-15):
1. Block the *LH* chord changes.
2. Play the *LH* as written. Play the down stem half notes *mf* and the up stem eighth notes *pp* and detached.

3. Work out the *RH* alone, counting aloud. (I suggest saying: "1-ee-&-duh, 2-ee-&-duh," etc. for each quarter note beat to be sure that all notes and rests are held for their exact value. Absolute precision is a must here!)
4. Play only the *LH* half notes with the *RH* melody.
5. Play as written with the upper and lower parts *mf* and the middle harmonies detached and *pp*. (This step is *for practice only* - certainly *not* for performance.)

Idea Two

In working out *idea two* (mm. 20-22):
1. Practice just the 4-note chords *f*, omitting the second eighth note of each beat.
2. Add the eighth notes, playing the chord tones *f* and the eighth notes, *pp*. *In performance, one must carefully avoid playing the repeated eighth notes f.*

Idea Three

In *idea three* (mm. 26-27), the LH should be played as *legato* as possible.
In working out these measures:
1. Practice playing the bottom notes alone, *legato*.
2. Then the play the upper notes alone, *legato*.
3. Play both notes, first broken from the bottom to the top, and then from the top down.
4. Play the 3rds as written, listening for *legato*.

- **Pedaling:** (See the reprinted full version for pedal suggestions) I always recommend adding pedal only when one is 100% secure playing the piece without it. For pedal practice, it is suggested that one first practice the *LH* alone plus the pedal prior to playing it *HT* with pedal.

Practicing the cadenzas (mm. 34, 44, 53, 87)

All but one of these cadenzas (the one in m. 53) are scored without bar lines, and are made of long strings of fast-moving 16th- and 32nd-note passages which utilize diatonic and chromatic scales, as well as diminished seventh arpeggios. These are all dramatic attention-getters and certainly illustrate the "free flights of fancy" which convey the piece's improvisatory character. Structurally, they also serve as bridges from one musical section to another.

Since most students will more than likely be working on this piece over a span of a number of weeks, they should have a variety of ways to approach the practice of the cadenzas.

PRACTICE SUGGESTIONS FOR CADENZAS (using measure 44 as an example)

1. "Accent" practice:
    - practice in accents of 1's, (placing equal stress on every tone);
    - in accents of 2's, (accenting every other tone);
    - in 3's (every third tone);
    - in 4's, in 6's and 8's.

2. "Backwards" practice:

(*I would suggest dividing this cadenza into two parts with the first part being from the high D# at the start of m. 44 and proceeding down to the lowest A in line 5; part two would begin on the next bass A, an octave higher, and proceed all the way up to the return of the A section in m. 45.*)

- begin by playing the last two *RH* notes before the *LH* low A in line 5;

- next, add on the preceding two *RH* notes, playing *G-F-E-D* plus the low *A*;

- for each subsequent playing, continue adding two additional notes onto the beginning of the passage until arriving all of the way back at the start of m. 44 (the high *D#*) and playing the complete passage down to the lowest *A*. etc.

3. Play in dotted rhythms:

and

4. Play the complete cadenza *very slowly*, *f*, and all detached.

5. Play in "impulses". (Always begin each impulse with the final note of the previous one.)

- Impulses of 4+1

- Impulses of 6+1

- Impulses of 8 +1

PRACTICE SUGGESTIONS FOR CADENZAS
(Descending scales in measures 34 and 44)

Play fast impulses stopping on finger 3 as shown in the following example taken from m. 34. (Always begin each impulse with the final note of the previous one. *Check to be sure that all fingers are always prepared for what follows.*)

PRACTICE SUGGESTIONS FOR CADENZAS
(Ascending scale in measure 87)

Play fast impulses that both begin and stop on the thumb.

Performing the cadenzas

Begin the runs in mm. 34, 44, and 87 somewhat slowly and with emphasis, and gradually *accelerando* to presto. (Since the diminished 7th passage in m. 53 actually comprises beats 3 and 4 of this measure, it should be played strictly in time.)

Note that at the end of the cadenza in m. 87, the 32nd notes change to 16th notes and then to eighth notes. Since this notation produces an automatic *ritard*, it is probably not necessary to also add much of a *rallentando* except perhaps on the last two notes.

Practicing the B section (mm. 55–end)

The LH Alberti bass patterns in the following excerpt are physically awkward and difficult to execute evenly because they occur in the middle of the keyboard and also include a C# to be played by the thumb. Elevating the wrist and tilting the *LH* slightly to the right towards the thumb will make this passage easier to play.

To ensure clarity and evenness, most students need ways to practice Alberti bass passages such as these. The following practice tips apply the suggestions made in Chapter 7 (using the Kuhlau *Sonatina* Op. 55) to mm. 79-81 of the *Fantasie*.

PRACTICE SUGGESTIONS FOR 16TH NOTE ALBERTI BASS PATTERNS

1. *LH:* block the three circled chords which appear in mm. 79, 80, and 81. *Observe fingering carefully.*

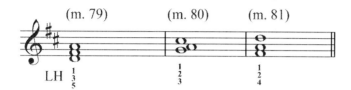

2. Practice the *LH* in accents of 2's, 3's, and 4's. *In order to ensure that all fingers receive equal individual attention, when playing accents in 4's, begin not only on the 1st note of each group of four notes, but also play 4's starting on the 2nd note, the 3rd note, and the 4th note of each group.*

3. Impulse practice for the *LH:*
    - play 5 notes *a tempo,* stopping on the last note. Always end each impulse prepared for what comes next. Begin each impulse on the final note of the previous one.
    - play each full measure, stopping on the 1st note in the next measure.

4. Slow, *f,* and detached practice. Play every *LH* note very slowly, *f,* and detached. *Be sure that all tones are equal in both volume and length.* Also practice it slowly, *pp,* and detached.

5. *HT:* When first adding the *RH,* play it very slowly and *mf,* and play the *LH* 16th notes detached and *pp.* (Note: This is for practice only – certainly not for performance.)

Performing the B section

Throughout the *B* part, the upper melody must always sing out over the *LH* accompaniment. As suggested above in step 5, playing the *RH mf* and the *LH* as softly as possible will help to produce this suggested voicing.

The rests and the change to *f* in mm. 86-87, plus the two fermatas in m. 87 must all be strictly observed. Note that no *diminuendo* is suggested at the end of the cadenza when the main theme of this part recurs. The abrupt changes from *p* to *f* and *pp* in mm. 94 to the end all add to the dramatic and improvisatory character of this piece.

In summary

The Mozart *Fantasie in D Minor* is a great "show-off" piece for a recital or contest, assuming that the student performer is up to both its technical and musical challenges which include much imagination and considerable refinement in terms of phrasing and voicing. Its musical content is extremely dramatic as well as sophisticated and subtle, all qualities which characterize much of the music of Mozart. Because it has so many different moods, it allows students to showcase not only their technical prowess but also their ability to play imaginatively and expressively. In my opinion, this piece is *not for everyone* — it takes a mature performer to "pull it off."

▶ FANTASY DANCE, OP. 124, NO. 5 BY SCHUMANN

FANTASY DANCE
(Opus 124, No. 5)

Robert Schumann
(1810-1856)

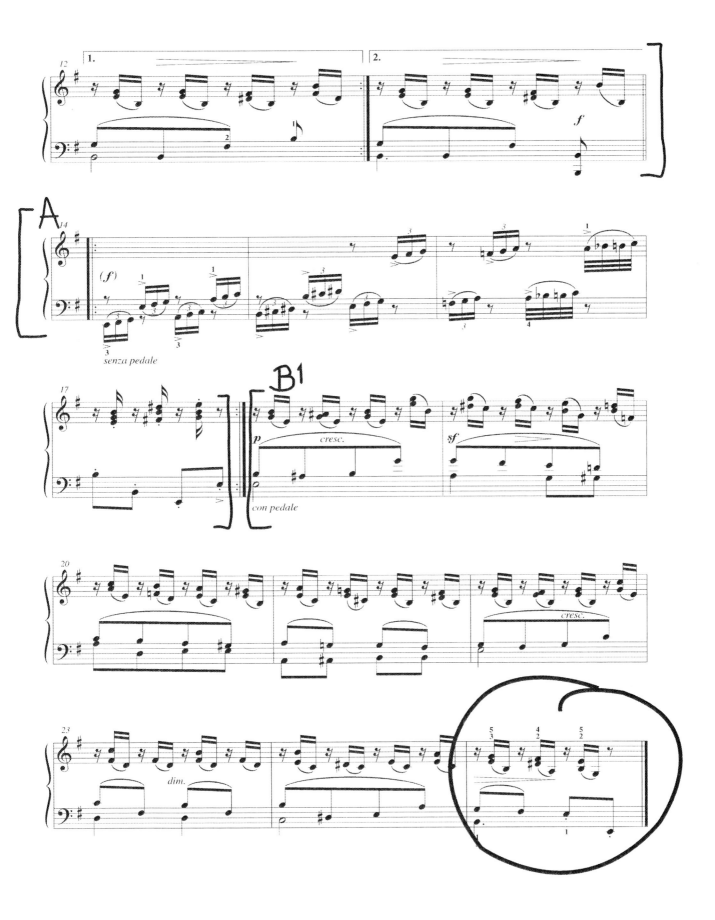

THE INITIAL PRESENTATION AT THE LESSON

Step One: *Discussing what the piece is about*

Unlike the Mozart *Fantasie*, this Romantic Era piece by Schumann does not display the "free flights of fancy" and improvisatory style characteristic of fantasies composed in Mozart's era. By Schumann's time, a "fantasy" had evolved into a "character" piece, usually short, and one which a composer could use as a vehicle of expression for every conceivable mood, thought, vision, or emotion. Schumann's use of the word "Dance" in this piece's title, along with the tempo designation of *Sehr rasch* (very fast) suggests a rapid dance, and, as such, its rhythm should be very exact and its tempo stable.

Step Two: *Hearing a performance of the piece* (as preparation for analysis)

As always, step two in the presentation of a new piece is to hear a performance of it. (As with the Mozart *Fantasie*, the student could listen to it on the CD that accompanies the *Festival Collection*, Book 6.) When played *a tempo* and with the suggested dynamics, the *Fantasy Dance* is very dramatic and exciting. Although certainly not easy, it tends to sound harder than it actually is. During my performance of the piece at the lesson, the student will, as usual, be asked to listen and follow the score in order to be ready for the next step — analyzing the piece's form.

Step Three: *Analyzing the piece's formal structure*

There are just two main ideas in the *Fantasy Dance* — an A section (mm. 1-4 which is repeated in mm. 14-17), and a B section (mm. 5-13 and its repetition in mm. 18 to the end.) Only the last measure is different from those of the first and second endings (mm. 12 and 13.) I would ask the student to circle this final measure as a reminder that it is somewhat different from the other two B section endings.

The analysis should also reveal that in the A part, the *RH* in mm. 1-3 copies the *LH*, and in the B part, the upper *RH* notes are the same as the *LH* melody found in the up-stem eighth notes.

Step Four: *The first week's assignment*

Since there are actually only 14 measures to learn (mm. 1-13, and then the last measure, number 25), a student should easily be able to work out the whole piece the first week.

SUGGESTIONS FOR PRACTICE AND PERFORMANCE

PRACTICE SUGGESTIONS FOR THE A *SECTION* (first week)

1. *HS* – using the "play-prepare" strategy, block the notes of each slur.

   LH blocks

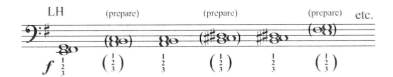

   RH blocks

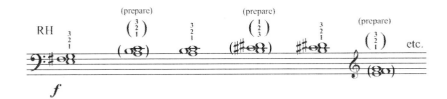

2. *HT* – play blocked, using alternating hands, i.e., *L, R, L, R,* etc., at ♩ = 50.

PRACTICE SUGGESTIONS FOR THE RHYTHM IN THE A *SECTION*

1. Set the metronome at ♩ = 52. With the metronome ticking, tap and count eight beats with one tap per tick.

2. With the metronome continuing to tick at ♩ = 52:
   • Subdivide into two eighth notes per "tick," and tap and count, saying "1 & 2 & 3 & 4 &," etc.

- Next, subdivide the beats into triplets, and tap and count.
  (When counting triplets, I ask my students to say, "one-uh-luh" because these syllables are so easy to verbalize. For counting 16th notes, I would suggest saying "one-ee-and-duh.")
- Finally, tap and count subdividing into four sixteenth notes on each "tick."

3. Still using the metronome tempo of ♩ = 52:
   Continue to tap and count, but randomly select different patterns, *i.e.*, begin with one tap per tick, then segue into four taps per tick, then switch to two taps per tick, then to threes, then back to fours, to twos, etc.

4. As soon as it is easy to keep a steady beat while arbitrarily moving from one of the above subdivisions to another, tap and count the actual rhythmic notation of the piece. The metronome setting of 52 now represents an eighth note (♪= 52; triplet 16th-notes and groupings of 32nd-notes are counted as in step two, *i.e.*, triplets and 16th notes.)

5. At the same metronomic tempo, play and count mm. 1-4 as written, dropping into each accented note.

PRACTICE SUGGESTIONS FOR THE B SECTION

1. *RH* chords, blocked: Play each chord and prepare for the next different chord. When secure, play as written.

2. *LH* – with suggested fingering, play only the *LH* up stem melody notes as *legato* as possible at ♪=52.

3. With suggested fingering, play only the *LH* down-stem notes (the bass progression) at ♪= 52.

4. Play both *LH* voices (the lower bass progression and the tenor melody) together as written, and as *legato* as possible.

5. *HT* – play *LH* as written, and *RH* blocked. Ignore the 16th rests and play each *RH* blocked chord simultaneously with each *LH* eighth note, ♪= 52, etc.

6. When step 5 is easy, play *HT* as written, counting the *RH* in triplets ("One-uh-luh, two-uh-luh," etc.).

PRACTICE SUGGESTIONS (after the first week)

To achieve a tempo:
Impulse practice – Play each beat plus the first note of the next beat.

When this is easy, increase the length of the impulse to a *whole measure* plus one note; then to *two* measures plus one note, etc.

To achieve evenness and clarity:
1. *RH* – Play *very* slowly (ca. 16th note =126 with one tick for each tone); play *f* and all detached.
2. *HT* – *RH* detached, *LH* legato as written.

Balancing the melody with the harmony in the B part:
1. At a *very slow* tempo, play only the *LH* up-stem melody notes *mf* and *legato*, and the *RH* as written but *pp* and detached.
2. Play *LH* as written and *RH* *pp* and detached (for practice only).
3. Play *HT* as written. Listen for the *legato LH* melody to sing out over the *RH*.

To technically coordinate hands together playing in the B part:
I have occasionally had students who have found it technically difficult to coordinate the *RH* with the *LH* in the B section because of the triplets entering after the 16th-note rests. The following practice steps have helped to minimize this problem, and they also make it easier to project the upper *RH* melody:

1. Play *RH* alone, *very slowly* and strongly accent the first 16th note in each group.
2. Play *HT very slowly*, continuing to accent the first *RH* note of each group.
3. Repeat step 2, gradually increasing the tempo; continue to accent the first *RH* note of each group.

Performance suggestions

- **Phrasing:** In the A section, I suggest thinking of bars 1-4 as one long 4-measure phrase. In the B part, I would once again phrase it in four-bar groups, taking a breath between mm. 8 and 9. Since the last eighth note in both the first and second endings is actually the upbeat leading into the next measure, there should be a breath before it as well. (*I ask my students to mark a √ into their score wherever a breath should be taken.*)

- **Dynamics and accents:** In the A parts, the placement of the accents is very important – especially the one that comes on the final *LH* note (the *E* in m. 4).

In the B section, I would encourage students to exaggerate the *cresc.* from m. 5 leading into the *sf* in m. 6, as well as the one that occurs in m. 9. In the latter *cresc.*, I would suggest going from *p* to *f* and then budgeting the *dim.* so that it doesn't arrive at *p* again until near the end of m. 12. In the 2nd ending (m. 13), the *f* leading to the return of the A section should be very sudden!

- **Pedaling:** This example shows some suggested pedaling for both the A and B parts.

In summary

Like the Mozart *Fantasie,* the Schumann *Fantasy Dance* makes a great recital or contest piece! But unlike the former piece, it is fairly straight forward and its performance does not require the same level of musical maturity and sophistication as the Mozart. By following the indications written into the score (the accents, *cresc., dim., sf,* etc.), most students who can handle its technical challenges at an appropriate tempo (ca. ♪= 176) should be able to create quite an exciting and dramatic effect with it. Students usually love this piece, and so do audiences. The *Fantasy Dance* provides lots of "bang for the buck" because it both looks and sounds much harder than it actually is!

▶ NOTTURNO, OP. 54, NO. 4 BY GRIEG

NOTTURNO
from *Lyric Pieces, Opus 54, No. 4*

Edvard Grieg
(1843-1907)

THE INITIAL PRESENTATION AT THE LESSON

Step One: *Discussing what the piece is about*

The Grieg *Notturno* is an excellent example of the 19th century "character piece" which became such a popular expressive vehicle for Romantic Era composers. By the time students are ready to play this piece, they would surely have already acquired the "dictionary habit," and hopefully they themselves would look up the word "*notturno*" ("nocturne") if they were unsure of its meaning. (*At this level, all of my students have their own music dictionary which they bring to their lessons, along with their music. They know that they are responsible for knowing the meaning of every word that appears in their pieces, and, whenever they encounter a new one, they are expected to look it up and then write its definition right on the score itself.*)

When the *Notturno* is first presented at the lesson, we would discuss some of the things which might be associated with the night, *i.e.*, a starry sky, bright moonlight reflecting on a pond or on white clouds floating in the sky, feelings of peace and calm, stillness, sleeping and dreaming, and yes, even the distant song of a nightingale. One might imagine the music of this particular nocturne describing a number of these things, and the student would no doubt also be able to add other imaginations as well.

Step Two: *Hearing a performance of the piece* (as preparation for analysis)

As with the Mozart and Schumann pieces, the student has an opportunity to hear a lovely performance of the *Notturno* on the CD that is included with Book 7 of the *Festival Collection*. Additionally, at the lesson I would play and "talk-through" the piece for the student as she listens and follows the score. We would note the peace and calm of the first idea (mm. 1-14 and its recurrence in mm. 34-54). The nightingale appears and sings its beautiful song in mm. 15-20 and again in mm. 55-60. What's happening in the third idea – the *piu mosso* (mm. 21-32)? There is certainly much more activity here! Perhaps this is a dream sequence which begins *pp* and somewhat calmly in m. 21, but at m. 29 climaxes into several measures of *ff*. The *dim.* and the *poco rit.* in mm. 31-32 suggest that the dream is coming to an end, and that wonderful measure of complete silence (m. 33) serves as the upbeat for a return to the peaceful beauty of the night that is experienced at the start of the piece. The second appearance of the nightingale (mm. 55-60) is followed by another measure of complete silence (m. 61), and the *Adagio* (mm. 62-63) provides a peaceful and beautiful ending for this night music.

Step Three: *Analyzing the piece's formal structure and marking and labeling its parts.*

The performance and "talk-through" of the piece should make it easy to determine where each major part begins and ends:

> A part – mm. 1-14
> B part – mm. 15-20
> C part – mm. 21-33
> A prime – mm. 34-54
> Coda – mm. 55 to the end (contains B part material)

Step Four: *The first week's assignment*

With most students I would probably assign just the A parts for the first week of practice.

SUGGESTIONS FOR PRACTICE AND PERFORMANCE
PRACTICE SUGGESTIONS FOR THE A PARTS

First week: HS only
1. *RH* – play the upper melody alone
2. *RH* (in mm. 8-13) – block as chords
3. *LH* – play the bass progression only (the lowest notes)
4. *LH* – block the chord changes (the harmony)
5. *LH* – combine the low bass progression with the blocked chords (the harmonic progression.)

Second week:
1. Review the *HS* practice steps assigned for week one.
2. Preparing for the 2 against 3 rhythm:
   • *HT, tap and count. Instead of counting it as nine beats per bar, I have my students count it in three's, and they say "one-two-uh-3" for the 2 vs. 3 patterns.*

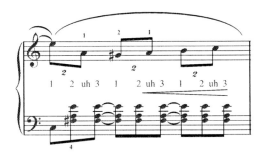

3. *HT* – When tapping and counting is easy, play and count (*very slowly!*).

   It is extremely important to continue on with the two against three counting ("one-two-uh-3") in mm. 51-54 to ensure that the basic quarter note pulse and its eighth-note divisions remain exact even where the eighth-note triplets are no longer present.

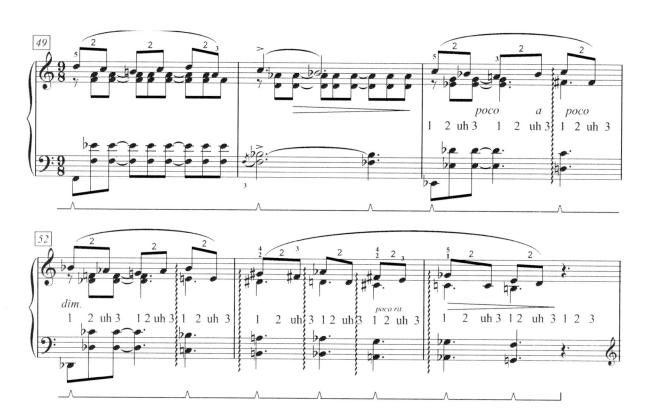

PRACTICE SUGGESTIONS FOR BALANCING MELODY WITH HARMONY IN THE *A PARTS*

1. Play *RH* upper melody with *LH* lower bass progression (omitting the harmony).
2. Play *RH* melody *mf* with the *LH* harmony. (Omit the lower bass notes and play just the *LH* chords *pp* and detached.)
3. Play the lower *LH* bass progression *mf* plus the chords (*pp* and detached).
4. *HT* – Play *RH* upper melody and bass progression *mf* and as *legato* as possible with the harmonies played *p*.

PRACTICE SUGGESTIONS FOR THE B PARTS

Practicing trills:

As a warm-up for the RH trills, set the metronome at ♪ = 72. Using the two trill fingers, play
(*p*) four beats in 2's, segueing into four beats of 3's, then 4's, then 6's, and finally 8's.

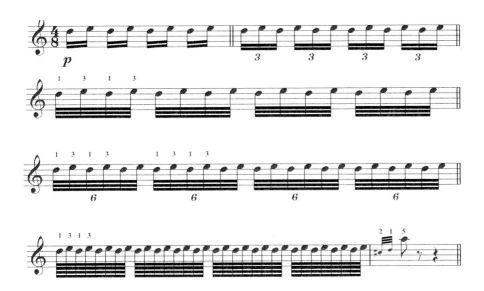

(*I find that trilling with fingers 3 and 1 in mm. 16 and 19 is easier than with fingers 4 and 3. I
suggest trying both fingering combinations and then selecting the one that feels the best. If fingers
1 and 3 are used, then the last three notes would need to be played with fingers 2-1-5. Because of
the A-flat in m. 60, this trill should be played with fingers 3-2 as indicated.*)

GENERAL PRACTICE STEPS FOR THE B PART:

1. *RH* – play and count as written.
2. *LH* – "play-prepare" the two chord changes.
3. *HT* – play and count as written.

PRACTICE STEPS FOR THE C PART

1. *RH*: Using the suggested fingering, play the *upper* notes only;

    then play the *lower* notes only;

    then play *both* notes *legato* as written.

2. Block the *LH*: Divide each group of four 16th notes into two parts (fingers 5-3 and fingers 2-1.)

3. Play *LH* alone as written. *To avoid stretching the hand, always rotate it towards the final note of each group of four notes.*

PRACTICE SUGGESTIONS FOR THE C PART (*after* the initial work-out)

For technical clarity and evenness:

1. *HS* – play each hand alone very slowly, *mf*, and detached.
2. *HT* – play very slowly, *mf*, and detached.
3. *RH* alone –

    play upper notes *legato* and lower notes detached;

    play lower notes *legato* and upper notes detached.

4. *HT* – play *LH legato* and *RH* detached; then play *LH* detached and *RH legato*.

To facilitate the LH "jumps":

1. Play all four notes of each *LH* pattern, stopping on the first note of the next pattern.

2. Play two 4-note *LH* groups, stopping on the first note of the next group of four.

Performance suggestions

- **Pedaling:** Suggested pedaling is shown in the following edited excerpt. For practice I would suggest the student play, at a *very slow* tempo, first the *LH* alone with the pedal, and then *HT* with the pedal.

- **"Terraced" dynamics:** In order to create the effect of a *crescendo* over an extended period of time, the dynamic changes must be budgeted. These must first be planned, the dynamic cues written into the score, and then practiced.

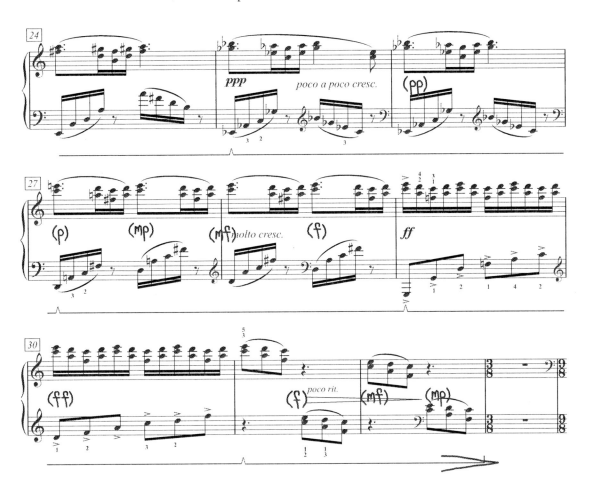

For practice, students should play each dynamic segment, pausing at the end of it to prepare for the desired dynamics of the next segment. Then the entire section (mm. 25-32) should be played in rhythm without pausing.

- **Crescendos in general:** In this piece, the performer needs to beware of creating textural heaviness in passages marked *cresc.* (mm. 9-14 and mm. 42-48). This can be avoided by minimizing the *crescendo* in the lower voices and letting the increase in sound occur primarily in the upper voices.

- **The significance of rests:** The three measures which feature silence rather than sound (mm. 33, 58, and 61) produce a truly special kind of accent. This silence should be felt as an upbeat leading into what follows.

In summary

What a glorious piece the Grieg *Notturno* is, and what wonderful preparation it provides for more demanding romantic "character pieces" such as the *Intermezzi* of Brahms, and of course, the *Nocturnes* of Chopin. But like the Mozart *Fantasie*, this piece is not for all students — even if they can play all of the notes at an appropriate performance tempo. In my opinion, it is only for those students who can not only handle its technical challenges, but can also do so in a highly imaginative and extremely sensitive and expressive way.

Preparing to Perform

Many believe that in order to really get to *know* someone, you need to actually *live* with them for a considerable length of time. I think that the same thing is true for a piece of music. Waiting until the last minute to get serious about learning performance pieces and then cramming to get them ready to play in public is unwise to say the least. But more important, such an approach seldom prepares a student pianistically, musically, or psychologically for a positive performance experience.

I think that the best performances are usually those of pieces that are thoroughly "seasoned." For most students, this entails beginning performance pieces far enough ahead of the actual date of the event to ensure total accuracy, technical control, and secure memorization. But equally important, the performers have to have "lived" with the music long enough to be able to form their own artistic judgment about it and then convincingly execute it at the keyboard, bringing to life what they believe to be the musical intent of the composition. This does not happen overnight — not even with extremely gifted "super star" performers who are able to read and play incredibly difficult music in record-breaking time.

I would classify most of the students with whom I currently work as "traditional" or average. All of them perform annually on at least one (but usually two) informal piano programs, one in mid-winter, and another in the late spring. I believe that participating in such events is an important part of each student's overall musical and pianistic education and that their purpose is to showcase the student's progress and ability to successfully make music at the piano — and to *enjoy* doing so! What I *don't* subscribe to is allowing preparation for performing (either in recitals or contests) to be the primary focus of lessons for extended periods of time. Although achieving readiness for successful performances should be the natural outgrowth of successful teaching, *it should never be the sole reason for teaching and certainly not a valid reason for parents to enroll their children in piano lessons.*

▶ PART I: PREPARING TO PERFORM IN STUDIO RECITALS

I avoid calling these events "recitals" because that word frequently seems to conjure up too many negative responses — often from transfer students who have had less than successful performance experiences in previous "recitals," and also from parents who, themselves, must not have had very positive recital experiences when they were children. So I choose to refer to these performance events as "informal piano programs" — *and informal they are!* The students all sit together in a semi-circle around the piano and I join them as the moderator. Not only do they each perform several pieces, but they also participate in discussions about the music and the composers; sometimes they get involved in an activity such as clapping an interesting rhythm pattern that might appear in one of the pieces; sometimes they are asked to tell the auditors what they like about the pieces they'll be playing; at other times, they might suggest one or two special things they would like the audience to listen for during their performance, etc. Because the environment for the program is very similar to that of their regular group lessons, they feel right at home. The only difference is that they are "dressed up" for the occasion, and there are a few more students involved as well as parents, relatives, and friends with whom they get to share their music-making.

In my studio we begin to prepare for a coming piano program several weeks prior to the event. The length of preparation time varies, depending upon the age and level of the student. For early-level young children, we usually start preparing around four weeks before the date of the program; older and more advanced students generally begin to prepare anywhere from six to eight weeks ahead of time.

Choosing the music

The first preparatory step is of course to select the repertoire. To get the ball rolling, students are asked to make a list of favorite pieces that they have thus far studied during the past 12-week term. They usually start out with between six to eight pieces on their list. I never pick their recital pieces for them. The only role I play in determining the selections is to specify that the pieces they choose should be ones that they really like and also which they think that they play really well (and with no inaccuracies or stumbles). I have found that when these are the criteria for their choices, they almost always make wise decisions. More often than not, their selections turn out to be the very ones that I would have picked had I been doing the choosing.

As soon as the student's list of "possibles" is complete, we hear all of the pieces at the lesson and over a period of several weeks, we gradually reduce the number of possibilities until we finally settle on the exact pieces which will be performed — usually at least two contrasting solos and one duet. This final decision generally happens about two to three weeks before the date of the program, and, from this point on, the primary focus of the lesson will be on "polishing" the repertoire, along with making suggestions for practice strategies that will maintain both the security and musical interpretation of each piece until its actual performance.

Maintenance practice

Most students enjoy the experience of playing for others when they are well prepared and successful. The only downside of performing is that they must continue to prioritize their performance pieces in their practice until the day of the program. Herein lie several dangers:

- becoming burned out and bored with the pieces,
- "peaking" too soon before the program, and
- assuming that since they already know the pieces very well, they no longer need to work carefully on them.

The student's obvious challenge is twofold — to avoid the above as much as possible while at the same time remaining in complete control of every aspect of the pieces slated for performance. The secret of staying interested is, of course, having great variety in how they approach these pieces when they practice them. We call this final phase of preparation "maintenance practice," and listed below are a number of ways to work on performance pieces which will help to prevent burnout and boredom, while, at the same time, ensuring retention of security and musicality.

MAINTENANCE PRACTICE TIPS

1. Three or four times during the week, do a complete play-through of the performance pieces and record them as you do so. *Keep going no matter what happens!* At the end of the performance, play back the recording as you follow the score and stop and work on any spots with which you were not satisfied.

2. Three or four times a week, set the metronome at a *super slow tempo* and play the whole piece *with* the music. (If the piece is long, I ask students to play just one part of it a day as suggested, and rotate its sections so that they have played the whole piece slowly and with the music at least once over the course of every 2-3 days.)

3. At least once a week, do a play-through of each solo for one or more members of your family or for a friend.

4. *Every* day work on any passages in your pieces which you think are challenging. Use a variety of approaches, i.e., one day, practice in accents; another day, do "backwards" practice, or hands separate practice; or impulse practice; or practice the passages slowly, f and detached, etc.

5. Several times during the week, play the *last* section of your pieces *first*, then play the middle section, and end with the first section.

6. If the piece is to be performed from memory, *every* day play at least its final measures *without the music*.

Obviously students would never do all of the above steps every day, or even every week. The point is that there must be enough variety in their practice strategies to ensure that they remain interested in continuing to *work* on their performance pieces rather than just playing through them. (The latter approach is dangerous because it almost always guarantees that a piece will begin to self-destruct before the performance date.)

Maintenance practice to retain secure memorization

In my own studio's informal piano programs, each student decides whether or not to play from memory or with the music. If a piece is to be played from memory, then, in addition to the above, the student's "maintenance practice" must also include regular "memory checks" to be sure that the memorization remains secure. Here again, to encourage continuing practice in this area, there must be a considerable variety of suggested approaches. I have listed a few of these below.

MEMORY CHECKS (FOR MAINTENANCE)

Be able to:

- play the piece(s) super slowly *without* the music.

- play either hand alone *without* the music.

- play the ending measures of the piece. *This is to ensure that no matter what happens along the way – even if one should get stuck and simply can't get back on track, at least one can always end the piece!*

- begin at any designated section *without* looking at the music. (With longer and more difficult pieces, we divide them up into numerous starting points and label them "1", "2", "3", etc. Then the student writes each number on a separate slip of paper and randomly draws from these to see if he can begin at that section without the music. I also use this procedure at the lesson to test them.)

- arbitrarily stop at any spot, get up from the piano, walk around a bit, return to the piano, and then continue on, starting on the very next note(s) from where you left off. (When we do this at the lesson, I often try to disrupt the student's concentration by engaging her in conversation while she is away from the instrument, *i.e.*, "What's your favorite subject in school?" "What's on your agenda for this evening?" "What's your favorite snack food?" etc.)

It is important that all memorized pieces are also played regularly *looking at the music* because this re-programs the visualization of the details. This "practicing-with-the-music" step should always be done *very slowly* — sometimes with the addition of all of the musical details (dynamics, pedaling, *ritards, accelerandos, fermatas*, etc.), and sometimes *without* these details, just playing slowly and without any pedal, and all at one dynamic level (perhaps *mf).*

I ask students to always bring their music to the program even if they plan to play without it. During the program, they "store" it underneath their chairs. Although I would *never* suggest to students that an unexpected memory mishap might derail their performance, still, if such should happen and they have their music with them, they can always just open it up and have a successful performance in spite of it. *(In all of my years of teaching, the need for this has only happened to a student once in a program, but believe me, that student was very glad that she had her music with her! Because of this, she was able to "save face" and her performance with the music was excellent and enthusiastically received by the audience.)*

Preparation for performance would also always include "trying out" the pieces in informal settings such as group lessons attended by peers, or in overlapped lessons with another student, or for family members, etc.

Recital decorum

As teachers, we should all be concerned about professionalism (or *lack* of it), and if so, then we, ourselves, must be responsible for establishing standards not only for how our students perform in public events, but also for their decorum *when* they perform.

Proper recital decorum includes knowing:

- how to walk to the piano (*briskly and with enthusiasm!*),
- how to adjust the bench,
- how to begin with the hands in the lap and take adequate time to *think* (and *breathe!*) before beginning,
- how to remove the hands from the keys at the end of the performance,
- how to bow (either a "sit-down" bow between pieces if the audience applauds, or a "stand-up" bow at the end), and
- how to leave the platform.

None of these things comes naturally. They all must be practiced until the student both looks and feels perfectly at home with them. *In addition to rehearsing all of the above in individual lessons, the group lesson format also provides a perfect forum for practicing them. Students are apt to feel much less self-conscious about these procedures when they observe their peers also doing them.*

Whenever possible, it's wonderful if students can have a brief rehearsal in the recital hall on the actual piano which they will be using for the program.

"Dressing" for the occasion

Not only are we living in a very fast-paced world but also one in which casualness seems to have become the accepted mode for both conduct and attire. I recall when I once observed a university string teacher at a recital of his pre-college level violin students. He was dressed in blue jeans, a sweatshirt, and well-traveled sneakers. And of course, most of his student performers were also similarly dressed. *(What a surprise!)*

In my opinion, knowing how to appropriately dress for a recital performance is an important part of recital decorum. Even though a program's format may be informal, it is still a special occasion and therefore students should be expected to dress for it. (Absolutely no flip-flop shoes, jeans, T-shirts, athletic shoes, etc. Girls must be especially careful about the height of the heels of their shoes if they are using the pedal and should actually practice while wearing the shoes they plan to wear when they play. And if they are going to wear a floor-length dress, it is also wise to rehearse walking, sitting down, and pedaling while wearing it.)

I believe that all student performances should be viewed as special events. Although the caliber of the actual performance in a recital is certainly the most important issue, surely "dressing up" for the event helps to make it seem even more "special" — both for the performers as well as for the audience. For this reason, for my own studio piano programs (and every collegiate preparatory department recital with which I have been involved), parents always receive a reminder memo before the event about suggested attire for the student performers. Below is a sample:

> Student performers are expected to "dress up" for the occasion with girls wearing either a dress, a "fancy" pants outfit, or a skirt and blouse; and guys wearing slacks and a shirt (with coat and tie optional). *Please* — no flip-flop shoes, jeans, sweatpants, T-shirts, sneakers, or other sports attire.

To my knowledge, no one has ever complained about this policy – at least not to *me*. And they all respectfully comply.

"Building" the recital program

I once heard a highly respected master teacher suggest that a well-constructed recital program should always feature the most reliable and impressive performers at its beginning and end and then "bury" all of the other performers somewhere in the middle. *(We certainly hope that, in his recitals, there are never too many "bodies" in this "middle-of-the-road" burial ground!)* The individual who advocated this program structure said that he did so because he was sure that most of the people in the audience will only remember the beginning and the end of a program and forget all of the rest! *(I hope this is not so, but you will have to make that call.)*

I, personally, do recommend staying away from starting programs with the youngest students playing the shortest and easiest pieces. If variety is the "spice of life," it is certainly also the recipe for building interesting recital programs. I agree that programs do need to begin with competent players who will capture the attention of the whole audience, but these can surely be students of any age and playing music at any level. I think that a contrast of moods, styles, dynamics, and pyrotechnics should dictate the order of the programmed selections. I also agree that the last two or three students on a program need to be extremely secure and impressive so that everyone does indeed leave feeling very enthusiastic and upbeat about the program as a whole.

One last recommendation — after the last player has finished, I think that it is always a good idea to ask the whole group of performers to stand, face the audience, and together, take a final bow.

Miscellaneous decorum in the recital hall

Students are expected to arrive at the site of the program at least ten minutes prior to starting time *(and we do start on time!),* and to sit at the front of the hall in their assigned seat in the section reserved for performers only. Both students and their parents and guests know that they are expected to attend the *entire* recital program. (I think that the length of student recitals should *never* exceed one hour.)

In the printed program, always included is a request that audience members turn off their cell phones and also refrain from taking flash pictures, setting up and operating video cameras (except at the rear of the recital hall and away from all aisles), or doing anything else that might prove to be distracting to either the performers or to other members of the audience. If parents wish to take pictures of their child (as most of them do), we request that this be done *after* the event is over, and at that time they can even have the student pose at the piano for the pictures if they so desire.

▶ PART II: PREPARING TO PERFORM IN COMPETITIONS AND AUDITIONS

Actually, preparing to perform in auditions, competitions, or other important events is pretty much the same as preparing to perform in a studio recital. Certainly the decorum and performance standards should be the same, regardless of the type of event. (It is gratifying to know that many of today's professional teachers' organizations, as well as sponsors of auditions and competitions, adhere to a dress code similar to the one described above for student performers and include this information in their general rules and regulations. Frequently adjudicators are even encouraged to comment on student attire if they think that it is inappropriate for the occasion.)

There are, of course, a few differences in the preparation leading up to a recital as opposed to other performance events. Obviously in most contests, "winners" are selected and prizes awarded. Therefore, it is necessary that student entrants (*and* their parents) are psychologically ready to deal with the possibility that they may not be among the selected winners. Of course, if this is the case, it is normal to experience some disappointment, but all involved must understand that even though the judges' expertise is respected, still, their choices reflect only their *own* opinions — nothing more nor less. Different judges might indeed have totally different opinions, and even the very same judges might come to entirely different conclusions on another day.

If the judges write critiques, I strongly suggest that these be given first to the student's *teacher* rather than directly to the student. As a teacher, I always appreciate having the opportunity to study the comments myself before the student (and the student's parents) see them. This way I can be sure that their initial review of what was said can be as positive and constructive as possible.

In my post-contest discussion with students, I always begin by asking what they thought about their performance – "What things pleased you?" "What do you think that you might have improved upon?" "What did you learn from this experience?" "Would you like to enter other contests in the future?" etc. Then I offer my own opinions (assuming that I was able to audit the student's performance). Finally, we study the judge's critique sheets together. During this portion of our discussion, I think it's important to remain as objective and unemotionally involved as possible. If I agree with the judges' assessment of certain things, I say so; and if I disagree, I also say so. The primary thing I want the student to understand is that regardless of what the judges say, it's always a matter of opinion (even though it's an *informed* one), and, therefore, we have to learn to take what is said with a grain of salt and roll with the punches. Those who choose to enter contests must know that this goes with the "contest" territory; and, believe it or not, "the sun will come up tomorrow" regardless of what the judges say.

Finally, I think that it's important for students and their parents to understand the musical and educational value that participation in such events can provide. Hopefully, the experience can not only be instructive but also positive and enjoyable and can help students to grow, not only as musicians and performers, but also as *people* — regardless of whether they "win" or not. I believe that most students will realize the benefits of contest participation if they are always well prepared both musically *and* psychologically beforehand, and also *if their parents demonstrate a healthy and positive attitude about their contest participation.*

Some additional thoughts about the 21st century contest scenario . . .

I recently had lunch with a highly esteemed friend and colleague — a university professor who is a stunning pianist, and a superb musician. Among other things, we of course talked about piano teaching, both in generalities and also in terms of teaching in the 21st century. He told me that previously he had always enjoyed teaching a few gifted pre-college level students in addition to his college piano majors but that he no longer did so because he found so many parents of today's students to be too aggressive and too contest-oriented. I remember his sighing and saying, "Oh, those *moms*! ... I just could no longer deal with them."

Our conversation also included a discussion of the pros and cons of contests. His opinion was that more often than not, the main focus of many of today's competition participants seemed to be on demonstrating pyrotechnics rather than musicality, and that the winners were frequently those who played the most notes in the "hardest" pieces and played them faster and louder than anyone else. He felt that in this technological age, the climate of contests for young musicians had become more like that of a highly competitive sports event rather than a vehicle for promoting and recognizing artistic refinement and expression. He also expressed a fear that dedicated and gifted teachers were all too often being replaced by "coaches" whose time and effort was primarily devoted to getting students ready for the next contest event.

I heartily agree with this assessment of the status quo of the 21st century contest scene. Because of this, I think it's important to thoroughly discuss this subject with the parents of prospective students before enrolling them for lessons. Some of them may very well place contest participation (and *winning*!) as the top priority for their child's piano study, even if they won't admit it. If this goal is not compatible with a teacher's musical and educational philosophy, then parents need to be made aware of this *before* they enroll, and should consequently be advised to seek another teacher whose top priorities for their child's piano study will be the same as their own.

I have certainly had my share of experiences with "stage moms" (and sometimes even with "stage dads"). They rarely show much interest in what their child is learning about music or the value of acquiring the self-discipline which underlies effective practice; nor do they seem to care much about things such as music history, or theory, or about the importance of developing good sight-playing skills, etc. Instead, the two things that seem to matter most to them are contest entries and the level of difficulty of the repertoire that is being assigned. Unfortunately, this issue of needing to perform "difficult" repertoire has also pervaded a number of student competitions and sometimes even influences those who judge them.

Apropos of this, a number of years ago, the parents of two of my students (both age nine and transfers from two out-of-state teachers) asked me if their child could enter a competition which occurs annually in our area. Ordinarily I chose not to enter students in this particular event because of some reservations I had about the quality of its professionalism. However, in this instance, I reluctantly went along with the idea and agreed that these two students might participate.

For the event, both children played a mid-intermediate level solo. The boy received 98 points for his performance and the girl, a 99. Both students' critique sheets from their judge (and they had *different* judges) contained a number of worthwhile comments about their performances. However, on each child's evaluation form, their judge had written that the student might have won a first place trophy had he/she played *harder* music. Although it would have been perfectly appropriate for a judge to submit such a comment via a personal note to a student's teacher, in my opinion, it should *never* appear on their evaluation form!

Now, many years later, I still remember this incident and have cited it here not because the two students were not first place winners but because of the indiscretion exhibited by the two judges who actually conveyed their opinions about the chosen repertoire to the students themselves. At the time, I viewed this as an exhibit of lack of professionalism on the part of the adjudicators and I still do. (As an aside, the judges' comments were troubling to both the students and their parents. As a matter of fact, it actually resulted in one of the student's mothers deciding to seek another teacher – most probably one who would be willing to assign "harder" music!)

Without a doubt, we all know that judges can be influenced by the level of difficulty of the chosen repertoire, especially when well performed, and many times this does indeed seem to play a role in their selection of winners. Whether or not we agree with this practice, it seems to go with the territory. As we assist our students in preparing for contest participation, we should be sure they understand that in addition to their choice of repertoire, there are also many other important factors that judges consider when selecting winners. Hopefully those organizations which sponsor student competitions share this belief when they plan and administer these events and that those who are chosen to adjudicate will also reflect this same philosophy.

Speaking of "harder" music, as I think back over the years in my own studio, most of the students who have dropped out have indeed been transfer students, and one of the most common reasons for the drop was because they (and their parents) thought that they should be playing *harder* music. And furthermore, they thought that it was perfectly OK to publicly perform such music in school talent shows, in recitals, and even in contests, *regardless of how it was played*. Needless to say, my own pedagogical philosophy prohibits me from assigning music that I think is inappropriate for a particular student, regardless of the reason. To do so would necessitate lowering my standards and expectations for excellence and this, in my opinion, would be a no-win situation for both the student and for me.

I recall another contest-related incident involving one of my students and her mother. This was a lovely 11-year-old girl who was scheduled to enter a fairly significant area competition. It just so happened that the public schools' and my own studio's week-long spring break occurred three weeks before the date of the contest and consequently, the student would not be having a lesson during that vacation week. I was stunned to receive an email from the child's mother informing me that she had contacted another teacher (someone I didn't even know!) to "coach" her daughter on her contest repertoire during the vacation, and she hoped that this would meet with my approval.

My reply made it clear that I did *not* approve. I thanked her for at least telling me about it but expressed regret that she had gone ahead and made the contact with the other teacher before first discussing it with me. I said that her child was already beautifully prepared for the event and that if she did indeed need extra help, I would be the first one to say so and provide it. I also told her that in all of my years of teaching, I had always taken full responsibility for my students' preparation for special events like this competition and to the best of my knowledge no parent had ever felt the need to seek "outside" assistance from another teacher. I went even a step further to say that if a parent of a student who was currently studying with another teacher were to contact *me* and ask me to coach her child, I would *never* consent to do so unless the child's *teacher* had made the request, and even then, I would probably not do so unless the teacher and a parent agreed to also attend the lesson along with the student. The mother responded immediately, indicating that she understood my point of view and had decided to cancel the coaching session with the other teacher. After a one-week vacation (which can often prove to be beneficial for many students), the child had two more lessons prior to the contest and although she was not a top winner, she did receive a medal and much praise from both judges for her "outstanding" performance.

One final word . . .

Most of us are already aware that in almost every community there are teachers who "specialize" in producing contest winners. Their students usually play exceedingly well and are frequently the ones who do indeed win most of the awards in area contests. These teachers usually have long waiting lists and many of them will not even consider accepting a student who does not clearly exhibit contest-winning potential. Some of these individuals are fine teachers. But, some are not teachers at all. Rather, they are "coaches" who operate what I think of as "contest mills" whose primary goal is to grind out as many winners as possible during each calendar year.

In this latter category it is common knowledge, at least in the area in which I live, that some of these individuals do actually agree to "coach" students of other teachers without the other teachers' knowledge and/or consent. And some have even been known to audit competitions and then — *believe it or not* — approach parents of gifted student performers who work with other teachers and suggest that the student leave the current teacher and study with them. But, because it *does* happen, teachers who are not only dedicated to providing excellence in music education but are also striving to exemplify the highest level of professionalism in their own studios need to be aware of it and do whatever they can to expose and stop this type of behind-the-scenes, underhanded activity.

In summary

Contests can certainly play a useful role as part of a student's overall musical and pianistic education and growth. They provide specific goals and incentives, and students can frequently profit from the comments and suggestions of well-qualified judges. However, whenever *winning* contests becomes the primary purpose for either teaching or for taking lessons, it's the old "tail-wagging-the-dog" story all over again. In my opinion, those students who are consistently receiving a well-rounded education in music are the real *all-time winners!* Their lives will be richer because of this and their "prize" — a lifetime of enjoyment of music and of being able to make it themselves at the piano — is far more significant than the trophies, medals, or monetary awards they might receive as contest winners. In the final analysis, each of us must decide which side of this issue we are on and make this very clear to the parents of prospective students. Then, the ball is in their court.

PART TWO:
PROFESSIONALISM

▲ INTRODUCTION

Much of the following discussion of professionalism in the piano studio was inspired by a phone call I received from a former student — a young woman who had studied with me for a number of years prior to entering college as a piano performance major. Upon receiving her undergraduate degree, she had decided to pursue a career as a piano teacher and she wanted to know if I would be willing to meet with her to discuss how she might get started in this profession. As we talked, I discovered that although she had had a year of piano pedagogy in college, she actually knew virtually nothing about what to do to establish herself as a qualified professional teacher within a community.

I agreed to assist her in every way possible and we set a date for a meeting. Actually, we had numerous meetings, and what follows are some of the issues we discussed and some of the suggestions that were proposed for her consideration.

Getting Started

▶ WHAT IS THE FIRST STEP?

- Compile and duplicate a résumé which contains a photo as well as a listing of educational background and professional achievements (at both the pre-college and collegiate levels).
- Design and duplicate a professional business card.

Individuals seeking students should always have a supply of these two items with them at all times so that they may be given to persons who express interest in studying with them, as well as to persons who might be willing to recommend them to others.

▶ WHERE SHALL I TEACH?

At an area collegiate institution
(particularly one which has a division for both children and adult enrollees on a non-credit basis):

- Obtain informational catalogs from these institutions in order to become acquainted with the types of music programs which currently exist.
- Find out who heads up these programs and contact them about possible job openings. Try to arrange for a personal interview with such individuals.
- In lieu of this, at least seek permission to send them a résumé for their files, and accompany it with a personal letter expressing interest in being interviewed for a future position whenever an opening occurs.

In many schools, a live, on-site teaching demonstration would be part of the interview process. Should this not be required, it would be to your advantage to have available a DVD which displays your actual teaching of several students at various levels of advancement in both individual and group lessons.

At an area community or private music school:
(The same suggestions apply.)

At an area music store:
Many music stores maintain teaching studios and hire personnel to staff them. There is also a possibility that a store might rent out studio space. The obvious advantage of this latter arrangement over the former is that it provides the instructor with a higher degree of independence in determining policies, selecting students, choosing teaching repertoire, establishing the fees, etc.

At a church or private school:
Sometimes a church or a private school may have a room that can be rented for teaching. Should this be the case, one would of course need to carefully check out the premises, especially in terms of the privacy issue as well as the quality of the piano. It would also be a good idea to inquire about its maintenance, *i.e.*, tuning and repairs as needed.

In a home studio:
This is an ideal solution to the "where shall I teach?" question, but not all teachers who are just starting out live in a home where they can set up a studio. If one does indeed plan to teach at home, it is important to check the local zoning ordinances to be sure that operating a home studio is legally permissible.

A home studio also opens up the possibility of being able to claim tax deductions related to its maintenance, providing that the space is used solely for business purposes. This issue should be discussed with a certified tax preparer or attorney before filing a tax return.

In an apartment, townhouse, or condominium:
If one plans to teach in one of these types of dwellings, it is important to check with the landlord, superintendent, or homeowners' association to be sure that teaching (as well as practicing) would be allowed, and if so, during what hours? In addition, there is a need to carefully check the soundproofing of the structure to be sure that other residents will not be disturbed by the sound of the piano.

In the homes of students:
If one has an automobile, going to students' homes to give the lessons is another option. In this case, the lesson fee would need to reflect the amount of time spent in transit as well as the expenses related to the operation of the vehicle. Sometimes a teacher can use the home of one of the students as the site for the teaching of several other students, assuming that the environment

of the room housing the piano provides adequate privacy, and that the instrument itself is a good one. If one does teach additional students in the home of one of the students, some sort of a financial arrangement such as a tuition credit should be offered to the parent of the student whose home is being used.

▶ ACQUIRING STUDENTS: HOW DO I GET THEM?

Certainly word-of-mouth references provided by one's own students and their parents are the very best recommendations one can obtain. However, until an individual has become an established teacher in a community, here are some other ways to get the ball rolling.

Join an area music teachers' organization:
Groups such as the National Federation of Music Clubs or the Music Teachers National Association (MTNA) and their state affiliates welcome new members and can frequently provide valuable assistance to newcomers seeking students.

Many such groups maintain a teachers' registry which provides the public with information about instructors who have openings for new students. Such a group also often maintains a website address with information about how individuals seeking teachers may contact a member who may have openings for new students in his or her schedule. Getting to know the teachers of such a professional organization and participating in its group-sponsored activities is one of the best ways for a new teacher to obtain referrals from colleagues whose schedules are currently filled.

Become acquainted with supervisors and teachers of music in the area schools — both public and private:
Try to arrange a personal meeting with these individuals and provide them with business cards and a professional résumé. Most of them would be pleased to find out that you are available not only as a qualified teacher, but also as an accompanist both for school ensembles as well as for vocal and instrumental students when the need arises.

Visit the area music stores:
It is important to get to know music store personnel and to find out whether the store maintains a teacher referral list. If so, teachers seeking students should request that their name be placed on it, and by all means, should provide the store owner/manager with some copies of their résumé and business cards so that these may be given to any clients who request teacher referrals.

Become professionally involved in music activities within your community:

- Serving as an accompanist for church and school events as well as for local vocalists and instrumentalists is an excellent way to become known as a skilled musician and pianist.

- Providing background music for wedding receptions and other similar social events is another good way to advance one's reputation as a competent pianist.

- One should also be on the lookout for opportunities to perform publicly as a soloist with an important priority being the presentation of a well-publicized full solo recital as soon as possible. This might take place at a church, a school, a library, a music store, or any other meeting place such as a Women's Club building wherever rentals are allowed and of course, where a satisfactory piano is available.

Utilize other miscellaneous means for advertising:

- One can certainly post a business card on local bulletin boards at supermarkets, on church bulletin boards, etc.

- Many communities have organizations (such as Welcome Wagon) which assist newcomers in the community with locating businesses and individuals who can provide them with specific services.

- Members of other groups such as the American Association of University Women (AAUW) and women's clubs might also be willing to make available business cards and other information about piano teachers to those interested in finding one.

- A local Chamber of Commerce might also be of some help in this endeavor.

Newspaper advertising:

This is also a possibility for acquiring students, but placing an ad in the "want ads" section is not recommended. Instead, teachers seeking students should consider buying space for an ad that features a professional photo as well as highlights of some of their musical and educational credentials.

An individual website:

Many individuals also find the use of the Internet (a professional website as well as social media) as an effective means for publicizing one's credentials and other pertinent information for those seeking a music teacher.

▶ HOW DO I DETERMINE THE AMOUNT OF LESSON FEES?

The best way to decide upon lesson fees is to first find out what the average going rate is in the community where one plans to teach. If one affiliates with a local music teachers group, it is certainly possible to get an idea about area lesson fees by asking individual teachers who are established and respected members of such a group. Lesson fee information might also be obtained from personnel of community music stores or by checking out the fee schedules that are usually contained within the catalogs of area institutions which offer individual and group lessons for children and adults.

Teachers just starting out in a community should beware of establishing lesson fees that are considerably lower than the going rate, but they should also be careful not to price themselves out of the market by selecting fees that are considerably higher than this rate. It is always possible to raise one's fees after a reasonable length of time has passed. As a matter of fact, the fees of many well established independent teachers often reflect an annual cost of living increase.

▶ PAYMENT OF FEES

The receipt of tuition fees is handled in various ways by teachers. Some teachers bill by the term or the semester, others on a monthly basis, but almost all agree that charging "by the lesson" is not only unprofessional, but also financially risky since the teacher is only paid if the student appears.

In my own independent studio, I have always charged by the term. I divide the academic year into three twelve-week terms, and tuition is payable in advance by the term. I am convinced that parents who pay in advance and for more than a week at a time are more apt to respect the importance of their child's study and attendance of lessons on a regular basis.

Pre-enrollment Procedures

The enrollment of most students is preceded by a phone call from a parent or an adult student who is seeking a teacher. I never enroll a new student without having a personal interview with him/her, and if the student is under the age of eighteen, I require that at least one parent also attend the interview.

If I have openings in my schedule for new students, *before* scheduling a pre-enrollment interview, I try to get as much information as possible about the prospective student via the initial phone inquiry.

- If the student is a child, what is his/her age and grade in school?
- Is she a beginner or has she had previous study?
- If the latter, how many years of study has the child had, is she currently studying, and, if so, what materials is she presently using?
- How much daily time does she spend practicing the piano?
- Does the child also take lessons on another instrument which requires daily practice?
- What are the parent's goals for the child's music study?, etc.

Of course, the caller will also have questions for the teacher to answer. The two questions that are usually at the top of the list are — What do you charge for lessons? On what day and hour would the lesson take place?

But certainly there are also numerous other significant questions that must be discussed — things that I think all parents and prospective students need to know before they enroll for lessons with any teacher. Rather than trying to discuss all of these important issues over the phone, I prefer to mail prospective students a packet of the information I want them to have prior to coming for an interview.

▶ THE PRE-ENROLLMENT PACKET

The pre-enrollment packet for prospective students should include information about:

- *The teacher's credentials*
- *The studio calendar and policies*
- *Practicing*
- *Group lessons*
- *Curriculum and materials*

The teacher's credentials

I have always found it somewhat disturbing that those inquiring about piano lessons rarely ask me about my qualifications as a teacher. Therefore, among the items I include in this mailed packet is detailed information about my educational and pedagogical background as well as about my ongoing career as a teacher, performer, author, workshop clinician, and composer.

The studio calendar and policy statement

Also included in the packet are a studio calendar of dates and events for the academic year and a statement of the studio policies. Over the years I have found that having a clear awareness of such policies *prior* to enrollment helps to prevent many of the problems which can easily arise once the lessons have begun. Following are sample copies of both a calendar and my studio policy statement. The latter has served me well for a good many years.

CALENDAR for 2014-15

The school year is divided into three 12-week terms. The dates are as follows:

FALL TERM: Wednesday, September 3 through Saturday, November 29, 2014.
  Vacation: Thanksgiving – No lessons on November 26, 27, 28, and 29.

WINTER TERM: Monday, December 1 through Saturday, March 7, 2015.
  Vacation: Winter – December 22 through Sunday, January 4.
  (Lessons resume the week of January 5.)

SPRING TERM: Monday, March 9 through Saturday, June 6, 2015.
  Vacation: Spring – March 30 through April 5.
  (Lessons resume the week of April 6.)
  Note: Lessons falling on Memorial Day will be re-scheduled.

SUMMER TERM: The dates of the summer term will be announced in mid-April of 2015.

NOTE: Lessons falling on school institute days as well as on other school holidays (Columbus Day, Veteran's Day, M.L. King Day, and President's Day) will take place as regularly scheduled. (These school holidays as well as institute days may sometimes be used for make-up lessons as needed.)

Group lessons will begin in January of 2015 and specific information will be provided at the end of Fall term.

OTHER IMPORTANT EVENT DATES TO PUT ON YOUR CALENDAR:

Annual Sonata-Sonatina Festival at North Central College – Saturday, November 22, 2014.

Recitals: **Winter** – Saturday, December 13, 2014, at two o'clock.
       Spring – Saturday, May 16, 2015, at two o'clock.
       (Location of programs to be announced.)

North Central College's Annual Spring Performance Auditions: Usually in late May; exact dates to be announced in the Fall of 2014.

STUDIO POLICIES

ENROLLMENT: Enrollment is by the 12-week term only, or for the balance of a term if a student begins lessons after the term has begun.

FEES: *For new students* – To reserve a place in the schedule, new students must return a completed application form along with a Schedule Data Form and the full tuition payment within one week following the interview. *For continuing students* – Tuition is due and payable in advance at the beginning of each term upon receipt of the statement.

REFUNDS: If a student withdraws prior to the start of a term, a full refund will be made; if withdrawal occurs prior to the end of week four, a 50% refund will be made; no refund will be made after the fourth week of the term.

MISSED LESSONS: Any lessons cancelled by the teacher will be made up. Although refunds or credits are not given for missed lessons, private lessons missed because of illness may be rescheduled providing the teacher is notified at least *by noon on the day of the lesson.* Only *one* missed lesson per term may be rescheduled. (Make-up lessons must be scheduled prior to the end of the term in which the lesson was missed.) *The teacher is not responsible for making up lessons that are cancelled for reasons other than illness.* Missed group lessons will not be made up.

LESSON EXCHANGES: At the beginning of each term, parents will be provided with a studio schedule so that a lesson exchange with another student can be arranged if necessary. Whenever the parent/student knows in advance that a lesson must be missed due to school activities, family trips, doctor's appointments, etc., it is the parent's responsibility to arrange for a lesson exchange with another student and to advise the teacher of the exchange at least three days prior to the day of the lesson.

Frequent absences and/or requests for lesson exchanges may result in the need for permanently changing the day/time of the student's lesson, or even dropping the student from the schedule.

GROUP LESSONS: In addition to weekly private lessons, the study plan also includes regular group lessons beginning in January. *All students are enrolled with the understanding that they will participate in group (or "partner") lessons.* (There is no additional charge for group lessons.) Parents will be advised of the dates and times of the groups in early January. During group lesson weeks, the private lesson will be abbreviated as follows:

- *For students enrolled in 45-minute private lessons, the abbreviated length of the private lesson will be 30 minutes.*
- *For students enrolled in 60-minute private lessons, the abbreviated private lesson will be 45 minutes.*

PRACTICE: Students are enrolled with the understanding that they will practice a minimum of five days each week. The minimum daily practice requirements are as follows:

For students in grades 2-5:	30 minutes a day
For students in grades 6-8:	45 minutes a day
For students in grades 9-12:	60 minutes a day

It is highly recommended that the suggested practice time be divided up into several short segments rather than being done all in one sitting. It is also advised that students schedule their practice to occur at the same time(s) every day.

Students will be asked to maintain a daily written practice record to be signed by a parent prior to each lesson. *Students who are unable to fulfill the specified practice requirements on a regular basis may be dropped from the schedule.*

LENDING LIBRARY MATERIALS: Students may be loaned materials from the teacher's lending library at no charge. In the event that such materials are lost or seriously damaged, they must be replaced at the current price rate.

STUDENT PERFORMANCES: All students will perform in at least one piano program during the school year. Although most programs are conducted in an informal format, performers are requested to "dress" for the occasion. (It is suggested that girls wear either a dress or skirt/blouse, and that boys wear slacks and a sport shirt with jacket and tie optional. "Flip-flop" shoes, jeans, T-shirts, shorts, athletic shoes, and other sports attire are not considered appropriate.)

If students are invited to perform in venues other than studio recitals, it should be understood that such performances will always be discussed in advance with the teacher and will never occur without the knowledge and permission of the teacher.

NEW MATERIALS: Most of the time, the teacher will purchase whatever study materials are needed and parents will then be billed for these items.

PARENT MEETINGS, CONFERENCES, AND LESSON VISITS: The annual Parents Meeting will take place early in the Fall term. (Date to be announced.) Parents are encouraged to request a conference with the teacher whenever they feel the need to discuss the student's attitude, progress, or study plan. Parents are also welcome to visit lessons providing the visits are pre-arranged with the teacher.

Practicing

Because I believe that student success probably depends more upon how he/she practices than on any other single factor, this aspect of piano study needs to be thoroughly understood by both the student and the parent prior to enrolling for lessons. Therefore, I also include in the pre-enrollment packet the following essay devoted to this subject. Each fall, I also mail a copy of this document to all returning students as a reminder of the commitment to practicing which they are expected to make in regard to their continuing piano study.

ABOUT PRACTICE

by Elvina Pearce

As we begin another new school year, our thoughts are once again focused on the importance of regular daily practice as one of the most important criteria for student success. For all students, I recommend a minimum of *five days a week of practice*. Ideally, this will be a regularly scheduled event that takes place at the *same* time every day.

Beginning students in their first year of study should average between 20-30 minutes a day and I *strongly* recommend that this be broken up into several shorter segments rather than being done all in one sitting.

After the first year of study, my recommendations for practice are as follows:
 Students in grades 2-5 — a minimum of 30 minutes a day
 Students in grades 6-8 — a minimum of 45 minutes a day
 Students in grades 9-12 — a minimum of 60 minutes per day
(Here again, I always suggest breaking up the daily practice into several short segments.)

Students who are consistently unable to fulfill the above practice minimums may be dropped from the schedule.

Important considerations

- *Consistency in Regular Daily Practice*

Parents sometimes express concern because their child does not go to the piano without being reminded, and sometimes the student demonstrates resistance to this reminder. Lack of enthusiasm over daily practice is quite normal for almost all students, regardless of age — and this is true even for those who might eventually choose music as a career. Nonetheless, since consistency in daily practice is perhaps the single most important element which influences student success, the parent should be willing to assume the responsibility for seeing to it that the child does indeed get to the piano at least five days a week. (Students are asked to maintain a written practice record each week which is to be signed by a parent prior to returning it at the next lesson.)

- *Practicing at the Same Time Each Day*

Students will be more apt to fulfill the goal of regular daily practice without undue pressure from a parent if a set time for daily practice has been established. My experience confirms that those students who practice at the *same time* every day tend to make better and more consistent progress than do those who use the "catch-as-catch-can" method of going to the piano. If your child has not yet established his/her special time for daily practice, you are encouraged to assist with this endeavor. (The student might wish to "try out" several different times for one-week periods and then select the time that seems to best suit both the student and the family's schedule.) Once the regular practice time has been selected, then the parent should be sure that the student sticks to it! Once practice has been programmed into specific time slots each day, I guarantee that there will be far less friction over this matter!

- *A Good Environment for Productive Practice*

Another important consideration about practice is that when the student is practicing, he/she is allowed access to the piano *without undue distractions* such as sounds from the TV, radio, or CDs, or from telephone calls, or from frequent interruptions by other family members. The point is that if practice is to become important to the student and a regular part of his/her daily routine, then a suitable environment for it must be created and respected by the entire family. This indicates to the student that all members of the family respectfully support its importance.

In summary

Finally, although consistent progress does depend upon time spent at the piano, I think that it depends even more upon *mind* spent while there, and consequently, this is always one of the main emphases of every lesson. Actually, most of each lesson is spent preparing the student for six days of productive self-directed practice between lessons. In order to reinforce what was done at the lesson, it is the teacher's responsibility to structure the student's assignment in considerable detail in order to reinforce the idea that practice is not simply sitting at the piano mindlessly playing through pieces. Rather, it's about understanding and utilizing practice strategies in a logical step-by-step sequence, and doing only those things that will ensure maximum accuracy and success with a minimum amount of time and effort.

Important practice suggestions are recorded in the lesson. Without a doubt, those students who review the audio/video recording return to the next lesson better prepared than do those who do not. Parents are also encouraged to listen to the recording in order to better comprehend each week's practice goals.

As previously stated, your child's success probably depends more upon *how* he or she practices than on anything else. This is what defines the quality of a student's accomplishments as well as attitude about continuing study.

Group lessons

Since my curriculum for students includes group lessons in addition to the weekly individual lesson, I think that it is important for new students and their parents to receive information about these classes. The packet that I mail out prior to the pre-enrollment interview contains the following essay on this subject.

WHY GROUP LESSONS?
by Elvina Pearce

I am sure that parents whose children have previously participated in group piano lessons are already as sold on their value as I am. Be that as it may, once each year, I like to review some of the advantages of this format, particularly for the parents of my new students. Below are a few of the reasons why I believe that all students should be involved with regular group instruction along with their individual lessons.

- **Group lessons provide a ready-made audience for regular performance opportunities.** We know that the more a student plays for others, the more he/she will feel at ease about performing, particularly if most of the performance experiences are for peers in a pleasant, non-threatening environment as opposed to the more "formal" recital setting. (When we are preparing for a recital performance, the group format also provides a perfect setting for rehearsing recital protocol, *i.e.*, walking to the piano, adjusting the bench, beginning and ending with the hands in the lap, bowing, etc.)

- **Group lessons provide valuable learning incentives.** Via performance experiences with peers at group lessons, students can gain learning incentives that cannot be provided as effectively by just the teacher. For example, when students hear the teacher play one of their pieces, they are not necessarily motivated by how well it is played. They expect that it will probably sound better when a teacher plays it than when they do. On the other hand, when they hear one of their pieces (or similar repertoire) played superbly by one of their peers, this performance becomes a believable model — one which they feel is within the realm of their own potential. "If my friend, Mark, can play the piece this well, so can I!" This is the kind of reassurance that can seldom be provided as effectively by an adult performance.

- **Group lessons provide valuable opportunities for students to learn how to listen to music.** In my own studio classes, we spend about 75% of the time making and listening to music (the remaining 25% being devoted to other miscellaneous activities). The students almost always follow the score as they listen, and we usually precede each performance with some sort of an activity which prepares the non-performers for active listening. For instance, sometimes I might assign each student something specific to listen for, *i.e.*, "Connie, you listen for dynamic contrasts." "James, please check the *staccatos vs. legato*." "Michelle, you check on the *ritards* and *fermatas.*" etc. Sometimes the non-performers are asked to study the music and then silently select one or two special things they plan to listen for. (In this case, the performer is not informed of these choices until after he or she has played the piece.)

Each performance is followed by some discussion. Sometimes the auditors are asked in advance to be prepared to discuss the piece's formal structure after hearing it (Is it ABA? etc.). Sometimes they are asked to mention one thing that they especially liked about the performance along with offering one suggestion for something that they think would make it even more effective. Once in a while, they are not allowed to look at the score as they listen but, instead, are asked to make a list of all of the things that they hear (*staccatos, ritards, crescendos, etc.*) *Who will have the longest list?* Sometimes they are asked to play "judge" and write out their comments. (In this case, I collect their sheets and then read all comments to the performer without revealing the identity of the writers.)

To encourage active listening, we always have to have something *specific* to listen for, and after each performance, we always evaluate it — "*Did we hear what we expected to hear?*" Pre-performance analysis of the music, following the score while listening, post-performance questions, and also other types of activities as mentioned above help to ensure that each of the auditors is every bit as involved as is the performer so that at *all* times, all are having a musical and educational experience.

A summary of the advantages of group lessons

- **Group lessons provide increased opportunities for ensemble playing.** All students enjoy being able to make music with their friends — playing either duets, or trios — or if there are two pianos in the studio, quartet music for four players. And what better place to do this than in a group lesson!

- **Group lessons provide more instruction time for the student.** For one example, in my own studio, the school year is divided into three 12-week terms, and most of my students are enrolled on a 45-minute private lesson basis. This means that during each term, *without* group lessons, these students would receive a total of nine hours of private instruction time. However, because group lessons are a regular part of the curriculum, the students will also have three one-hour group lessons per term in addition to their weekly private lessons. (During group lesson weeks, the private lessons are abbreviated, i.e., 45-minute lessons become 30-minute lessons. Making this change frees up time in the schedule so that it is possible to offer the groups.) The above plan means that during each 12-week term, my students have nine 45-minute private lessons (totaling six and 3/4 hours of time), three 30-minute private lessons (totaling an hour and a half), and three one-hour groups. This results in their receiving a total of eleven and a quarter hours of instruction per term as opposed to just nine hours were they to have only the twelve 45-minute private lessons.

- **Group lessons provide additional time for reinforcement drills.** It is very difficult to squeeze into a private lesson all of the drill activity needed to reinforce concepts being learned in the areas of reading, rhythm, theory, ear training, etc. Group lessons provide the perfect setting for such drills, and, of course, they are always more fun when done with peers rather than when done by just the student and a teacher at a private lesson.

- **Group lessons can provide a great forum for composing.** One emphasis in my own group lessons is on composing. For each class, students are asked to create a piece of their own based on a format assigned and illustrated at the previous class, i.e., "For next month's group, make a piece in which the left hand always plays only on black keys and the right hand, on white keys"; or, "Make a piece in ABA form"; or a piece that includes both major and minor; or a piece built around an *ostinato* figure, etc. It is always fun to hear three or four original pieces all based on the same structural format but with each sounding so different!

- **Group lessons can enhance intelligent practice strategies.** Sometimes I assign an "on-own" piece to everyone in the class — the *same* piece to each student. This is always a short piece that is at least a couple of levels easier than the students' regular repertoire, and one that I'm *sure* no one has ever studied. The idea is that each student is to work the piece out *entirely by him/herself*, write out the practice steps used, and then play it at the next class. We usually ask the student that is the best prepared to demonstrate the practice strategies that were used to produce his/her performance. (I believe that students can often learn just as much about effective practice strategies from each other as from their teacher.) As an aside, I also regularly assign "on-own" pieces to students at their private lessons as well as for a group assignment. This is about the best yardstick I have found for measuring what a student has *really* learned — and has *not* yet learned — about how to practice.

- **Group lessons help to minimize the solitary status that many students associate with piano lessons.** It's obvious why students enjoy singing in the school chorus or playing in the band or orchestra — because it's something they are doing with their *peers!* But what about taking piano lessons? The child who always has the lesson alone, and who is expected to practice alone can easily feel that this "piano" activity is outside of the mainstream of his/her life and can, therefore, be less motivated to want to practice and continue on with the lessons.

  On the other hand, students who regularly share the musical experience with others — particularly with their peers — have an opportunity to experience the same type of enjoyment that they receive when participating in group musical activities at school. This sharing can often make the difference between a decision to continue on with lessons or to drop out.

As we think about the many advantages provided by group lessons, it is obvious that they can add a dimension to music study that the private lesson by itself can never provide. Hopefully, more and more students are experiencing the adventures inherent in group lessons, and because of this, we are finding ourselves producing a generation of performers who not only play for others with more ease and enjoyment, but who are also able to intelligently, actively, and imaginatively listen to music as well!

Curriculum and materials

The pre-enrollment interview packet also contains some general information about the goals of the curriculum and the materials that will be used to achieve them. This will be discussed in more specific detail at the end of the interview itself, based upon the perceived needs of the student and whether or not the student is a beginner or has had previous study.

In summary

I believe that many of the problems that sometimes arise over the course of time could probably have been prevented had the parents and/or students been adequately informed of the important issues and studio policies *prior to enrollment*. I also believe that such information should be presented *in writing* and not by word of mouth. (I remember hearing Frances Clark frequently say, "If it isn't *in writing*, it doesn't exist!")

▶ PRE-ENROLLMENT INTERVIEWS

As previously stated, all prospective students are interviewed prior to their enrollment, and the interview of those under the age of eighteen must also be attended by at least one parent. I allow an hour for the interview and there is no charge.

Of course every interview begins with a "getting-to-know-you" segment so that all of us — parent, student, and teacher — can find out as much as possible about each other. Following this, the main emphasis shifts to the specifics of music and making music at the piano. Of course, the structure and contents of the interview with students who have had previous study ("transfer" students) is quite different from that of beginners.

The beginner's interview

With young children who have had no previous study, the main purpose of the interview is to determine whether or not the child is ready to begin "formal" lessons. To assist with this, I evaluate a number of things.

- First of all, I always ask the child if he can already play something on the piano, and, if so, of course I am eager to hear it.
- Another focus of the beginner's interview is to evaluate the child's aural awareness — the ability to identify high, low, and "middle" sounds, ascending and descending tones, loud and soft, long and short, and detached and connected sounds. Depending upon the age and maturity of the child, I sometimes also check to see if he can play back short musical patterns.

- Another issue to consider is rhythmic skills — marching to music, clap-backs, and/or playbacks of rhythm patterns, etc.
- Also evaluated is the child's physical maturity — the size of the hands, strength of fingers, body tension/relaxation, and coordination.

In addition to the general things mentioned above, I think that the most important thing I do in a beginner's interview is to teach the child by rote to play several pieces. This provides *specific* information about his physical coordination, strength of the hands and fingers, rhythmic stability, attention span, and also the ability to comprehend and apply new concepts at the keyboard. More than anything else, the information I gain in the "teaching" segment of the interview helps me to determine if I think that the child is ready to begin formal piano study.

Prior to the interview, the parent has already been provided with comprehensive printed information about my approach to teaching beginners — my goals for their first year of study, and the materials that will be used to fulfill them. The conclusion of the interview presents an opportunity to discuss this as well as any other things about which the parent might have questions.

The "transfer" student's interview

Prior to the interview, the initial phone contact with the parent has already provided a lot of information about the student — her age, grade in school, length of previous study, and the repertoire most recently studied. I ask the student to bring to the interview all of the materials that have been assigned and worked on during the past twelve months. In addition, I would also like to see all of the miscellaneous collections of piano music which the student has but has not yet completed. All of this information is recorded on the student's interview form.

For the interview, I request that the student be prepared to play three favorite pieces. (Ideally, I would hope that one of these might be a piece that the student has worked out on his own without the help of a teacher.) I emphasize that the pieces need not be memorized, and that the student does not necessarily have to play all of each piece. I just need to hear enough of it to give me an idea about her accomplishment — accuracy, musicality, pedaling, technique, etc. Prior to playing the audition pieces, I suggest that the student first "try" the piano by doing some sort of a technical warm-up — a scale and/or an arpeggio if these have been studied — and I also record this data on the interview form.

Before hearing each piece, I like to find out how long the student has been working on it, and I frequently ask questions about the piece's composer, its form, its key, its mood, the meaning of some of the Italian terms found in the music, etc. After hearing whatever pieces the student has selected to perform, I always choose at least one of them and work a bit on it with the student just as we might do at a lesson. This not only gives the student and parent a preview of what might take place at lessons, but it also provides me with valuable information about how flexible the student is in terms of assimilating new ideas into a performance, *i.e.*, "Try playing it at this slightly faster (or slower) tempo." "Play this section again and this time, strive to project a lot more exaggeration of all of the dynamic changes." "Let's see if you can play the left-hand accompaniment less loud in this section," etc.

By the time the performance segment of the audition is over, I should have at least a tentative plan for what needs to be done in the areas of technique, theory, musicianship, and work habits, and I will also have some ideas about what specific repertoire to assign. All of this data is recorded on the interview form, and it is also discussed with both the student and parent.

Sometimes the interview convinces me that I would not be the "right" teacher for a particular student. For one example, I remember interviewing a very bright fifteen-year-old boy who had a considerable amount of technical facility and obviously much musical potential. However, during the interview it became quite clear that his interest was to play *only* jazz and "pop" music on his electronic keyboard. (I found out that the family did not even own an acoustic piano.) Consequently, instead of enrolling this student, I gave him names of several teachers that I thought could really assist him with fulfilling his musical and pianistic goals. (Sometime later he wrote me a letter telling me how much he was enjoying his piano lessons, and thanking me for my teacher recommendations.)

Once in a while with a young beginner, I decide that he is not yet ready to begin piano study and would profit by having some sort of a "pre-piano" musical experience as readiness for more "formal" study. (*I remember interviewing one young child who preferred to lie in the fetal position on the small couch in my studio during most of the interview. Although he might have been ready for a nap, I was reasonably sure that he was not ready to begin formal piano study and that he might not even have been ready for enrollment in a "pre-piano" course!*)

On a few occasions, I have met prospective students who exhibit very negative attitudes about taking lessons, fulfilling the daily practice requirements, etc. Experience has taught me that enrolling such a student is quite often a no-win situation for both the student and for me as well.

The long and short of it is that if, on the basis of the interview, I decide to *not* accept a student for lessons, then, of course, this must be discussed with the parent, complete with my reasons for arriving at this decision. This discussion might take place in the presence of the student, but I much prefer to do it either by phone or in a separate meeting with the parent so that we may talk candidly without the student's being present.

The application form

Assuming that the student is accepted for lessons, then the last thing that is done at the interview is to provide an application for study and a data form to be used for scheduling purposes. I always encourage the parent/student to not "sign up on the spot" at the interview, but rather to sit down at home and seriously discuss all of the implications of enrolling for lessons in my studio. If, after "sleeping on it," they decide to enroll, then they are asked to complete the application and scheduling forms that follow, and return them, along with the specified tuition payment within one week following the interview.

APPLICATION FOR STUDY

Name of Student: _____

Address: _____
       Street   City   Zip Code

Student's Age _____ (As of Sept., 20__)   Grade in School_____ (As of Sept., 20__)

Name of School: _____

School dismissal time: _____

Name of Parent:_____ Home Phone: _____

Cell Phone:_____ Home E-mail Address: _____

Is student a beginner? _____Yes _____No   If no, years of previous study: _____

If student has had previous lessons, please list below the books/pieces studied most recently:

_____
_____
_____
_____

Desired length of lesson:_____   Date of 1st lesson: _____

Signature of Parent: _____ Date of Application: _____

About Tuition

The school year is divided into three 12-week terms. The summer term is for six weeks. Tuition is due and payable in advance at the beginning of each term upon receipt of the statement. Tuition for each 12-week term is as follows:

On a weekly 45-minute private lesson basis: $_____

On a weekly 60-minute private lesson basis: $_____

To complete enrollment and reserve a place in the schedule, please provide the information requested on both sides of this application form and return it, along with the tuition fee of $_____ on or before _____.

Please also provide the following information about the student:

1. If, in addition to piano lessons, the student will also be taking (violin, oboe, voice, etc.) lessons, approximately how long each day will the student spend practicing this instrument? _____ minutes

2. Is the student enrolled in any school "honors" classes? If so, which ones?
_____

3. The student spends approximately how much time each day doing homework?   _____ minutes.

4. Is the student involved in any school clubs? If so, which ones and when do they meet?
_____
_____

5. Is the student enrolled in one of the school's music programs? (orchestra, band, chorus?) If so, which one(s)?
_____

6. List below other activities that are a part of the student's regular daily/weekly schedule. (soccer, cheerleading, badminton, swimming, tennis, etc.)
_____
_____

(Please attach a copy of the schedules of games and of after-school practice to the application.)

7. List regular weekly activities that are not sponsored by the school. (Scouting, swimming lessons, ice skating, karate lessons, a regular church group meeting, etc.). When and for how long is each activity? (Example: Karate - Wednesdays from 5:00 to 6:00.)
_____
_____

8. At what time of day does the student generally practice the piano? _____

If there is any other information that you would like to provide about the student, please include it on an additional sheet and attach it to this application form.

The schedule data form

Setting up a studio schedule in today's world in which both parents in a family often work and where most students are over-scheduled with multi-curricular activities can be both time consuming and frustrating. It is not at all unusual to have students who can provide only one or two time slots during a whole week when they can actually come for a piano lesson. Years ago, I learned that setting up my own teaching schedule is considerably easier if I never solicit the information I need for scheduling over the telephone. Nor do I accept such information via a phone call from students or parents. Instead, I request that all pertinent information be submitted in writing on a Schedule Data Form such as the one shown below.

New students who are accepted for lessons receive a copy of this scheduling form along with an application for study at the conclusion of their pre-enrollment interview. A similar scheduling form is mailed to all returning students about one month prior to the start of each new academic year. (The reverse side of this form for returning students includes essentially the same questions as those that appear at the end of the new student application form.)

SCHEDULE DATA FORM

Schedule Data Form for: _____
(Name of Student)

Place an X in all time slots when it would not be possible to be scheduled for a lesson. Return this form, along with a check for the designated tuition no later than _____.

Please include information for all 6 days. (It is important that you indicate possible lesson times for at least 2 different days during the week.)

Preferences
1st choice of day and hour _____
2nd choice of day and hour_____

(Note: Preferences are considered on a first-come, first-served basis. However, it should be understood that it is not always possible to honor all special requests.)

	MON	TUES	WED	THUR	FRI	SAT	
2:45						9:00	
3:00						9:15	
3:15						9:30	
3:30						9:45	
3:45						10:00	
4:00						10:15	
4:15						10:30	
4:30						10:45	
4:45						11:00	
5:00						11:15	
5:15						11:30	
5:30						11:45	
5:45						12:00	
6:00							
6:15							
6:30							

Name of parent: _____
Home address:_____ Home phone: _____
Work phone: _____ Cell phone: _____ Email: _____

The scheduling, assignment, and notification of lesson times

The Schedule Data Form must be returned no later than ten days prior to the starting date of lessons. Once forms have been received from all students, then the schedule is made and within 24 hours, each parent is notified of the day and hour of the student's lesson *in writing* via the email memo that follows.

MEMO TO PARENTS ABOUT LESSON SCHEDULE ASSIGNMENT

Date: _____

Based on the information that you provided on the Schedule Data Form, _____'s piano lessons for this year have been scheduled for _____ from_____ to _____o'clock.

The first lesson will be on _____.

Note: *In the event that the above assigned day and hour is not possible, it will be the parent's responsibility to contact the teacher for information about how to arrange for an exchange of lesson times with another student.*

For the first lesson, the student should bring:
1. An audio or video recording device
2. A 3-ring, loose-leaf binder notebook
3. All of the music books and other materials used during the previous six months.
   (If new materials are assigned, these will be billed after lessons begin.)

A REMINDER ABOUT THE POLICY FOR MISSED LESSONS
As explained in the studio's policy statement, no refunds or credits are given for missed lessons. Any lesson(s) cancelled by the teacher will be made up.

A private lesson cancelled because of illness will be made up if the teacher is notified by noon on the day of the lesson.

Only *one* make-up lesson per term may be scheduled, and this must take place during the term in which the lesson was missed. Make-ups for missed lessons in a term will *not* be carried over into the next term. Whenever possible, make-up lessons may be scheduled on a school holiday (such as teacher institute days, Columbus Day, etc.).

LESSON EXCHANGES
Several weeks after the term begins, parents will be provided with names, phone numbers, and the day and hour of lessons of students with whom lesson exchanges might be arranged should this become necessary.

If a student must miss a lesson for reasons other than illness (a doctor's appointment, field trips, a play rehearsal, sports events, and other miscellaneous school and social activities), it is the parent's responsibility to arrange in advance for a lesson exchange with another student and to advise the teacher of this exchange at least *three days prior* to the day of the lesson.

Summary remarks about scheduling . . .

Once the scheduling has been completed and the above memo to parents has been sent out, if the assigned day and hour for lessons is not agreeable, I am willing to provide the parent with contact information about other students with whom a lesson trade might be possible. But it is understood, that should a lesson change be necessary *after* the schedule has already been set up, *it is the parent and not the teacher who is responsible for arranging for the change.*

Each student's Schedule Data Form is kept on file and it is also used to establish the day and hour of group lessons (which begin in January), as well as for the scheduling of make-up lessons.

For what it might be worth, I have been using the Schedule Data Form "in writing" procedure for scheduling lessons in my own independent studio for more than thirty years, both for group and individual lessons. And as the director of several large institutional preparatory departments involving numerous staff members and hundreds of students, I have also advocated its use in those programs as well. This procedure makes short order of trying to assign workable lesson times and takes virtually all of the hassle out of scheduling. It usually works like a charm!

Professional Decorum

▶ PROFESSIONAL DECORUM IN THE STUDIO

The teacher's attire

I believe that what a teacher wears when students and their parents are present is important in establishing a level of professionalism in the piano studio. Although some degree of casualness is certainly acceptable, good taste should always be the rule. (I, personally, do not think that the wearing of blue jeans and other similar clothing is appropriate teaching attire.) If we want every piano lesson to be a special event, then how we dress for it will undoubtedly help to facilitate this.

The studio environment

The environment of the site in which students have their lessons is also important. Surely a neat, clean, and well-organized space is more conducive to promoting concentration and a high quality of musical achievement than is a cluttered, disheveled studio. In addition, the "look" of the studio is certainly a visible part of the professional standards which teachers should be promoting. Apropos of this, I remember hearing about a pre-enrollment interview that a parent described to one of my colleagues. The parent said that during the entire interview, the sound of nonstop chirping caged birds (*obviously more than one*) was extremely disconcerting. She also said that after she and her daughter left the home, they discovered that they were both covered with dog hairs, no doubt having been deposited by the animal on the sofa on which they had been sitting. *Needless to say, the parent did not enroll her child for lessons with this teacher!*

Punctuality

I believe that punctuality is also an important component of professional studio operations. *Lessons should both begin and end on time.* I have found that students who tend to be chronically late for their lessons are more apt to arrive on time if their parents understand that the ending time of their child's lessons will not be extended to compensate for tardiness. Of course this works both ways. If we expect punctuality on the part of our students, then we, too, must also be punctual, ready to begin the lesson at the specified time, and making every effort to conclude it as scheduled.

▶ NON-PROFESSIONAL DECORUM IN THE STUDIO

I believe that for maximum learning, students need to receive 100% of the teacher's *uninterrupted* attention for the entire duration of a lesson. If the things listed below are occurring during lessons, they are not only disruptive but could also be described as *non-professional*. (One would think that most of these things would probably only happen in a home studio, but not so. I have observed some of them also occurring in collegiate venues as well.)

Answering the telephone while teaching

Early in my teaching career I was pleased to have been given the opportunity of spending an afternoon observing the teaching of a highly respected piano instructor who was the head of a large preparatory division in a major university. I don't remember anything that I learned that day about teaching, but I do remember that there was a telephone in her studio and that during the course of the afternoon, the phone rang at least once during every lesson. Not only did the teacher answer it, but she also engaged in conversation with each caller as well. Although I was a young and inexperienced teacher at the time, I recognized that this occurrence seriously impaired the students' concentration and disrupted the flow and building of momentum in the lesson. And I also found myself wondering *"What kind of a message is being sent to the student who is left sitting at the piano doodling around while the teacher talks on the telephone?"* Of course, it is possible to turn off cell phones, turn on answering devices, and deactivate a standard home telephone. And this procedure should be part of the professional decorum of the teacher in every studio whenever lessons are taking place.

Answering the door while teaching

Leaving the student sitting at the piano while answering the door is just as disruptive and non-professional as is answering the telephone during lessons. If one expects deliveries, then a time frame can be established in advance as to when these may occur. Whenever I teach — whether in an institutional studio or at home — I always post a note on the door indicating that I am teaching and therefore presently unavailable. The note also includes information about both *when* and *how* to contact me.

Other disruptions of lessons

If one is teaching in a home studio, family members entering and exiting the teaching area while lessons are in progress would be a great distraction and certainly such occurrences will not enhance the image of professionalism. If one decides to teach at home, then all who reside there must understand and respect the fact that access to the teaching room is 100% *off limits* whenever lessons are in progress. Also, all residents in the home must understand the necessity for controlling the noise factor. Sounds from the radio, the TV, or from CDs, DVDs, and video games, as well as loud talking and rowdy activities taking place within earshot of the studio are not acceptable. If preschool-age children are present in the home, it is absolutely essential that their care be under the supervision of a responsible individual whenever lessons are being given. Although teaching at home can certainly offer a number of advantages for the teacher, it can sometimes also prove to be not so advantageous for the rest of the family.

Allowing pets in the studio

One would think that the presence of animals in a teaching situation might happen in a home studio but never within a collegiate environment. Not so! I remember in my first university position, I was walking down the hall in the music building one afternoon when I heard an instructor shouting, "GET BACK ON YOUR PAPER!!" I was so curious that I couldn't resist peeking in the small window of her studio door to see what was going on, and lo and behold, there she was, down on her hands and knees on the floor trying to persuade her pet dachshund to leave the student alone and get back on the newspaper that had been placed in a corner of the studio for obvious reasons. Here again, *this kind of an event is certainly disruptive and should never be taking place in a "professional" studio.*

Eating during lessons

Now here's one for the books! A student in one of my university "pedagogy 101" classes once told the class that his pre-college teacher had around 80 students a week and therefore taught almost around the clock — in the mornings before school, during the noon hour, after school, and well into the evening hours, and of course, nonstop all day on Saturdays. When the student asked the teacher if he didn't at least take some time out for a Saturday lunch break, he said, "Oh, no. I simply go behind my floor-length screen in the studio and eat my lunch there so that I can continue to teach." *How does such studio decorum contribute to the image of professionalism which most teachers think is so vitally important??*

In summary

For as long as I can remember, national music organizations have been devoted to upgrading the professional standards associated with music teaching, particularly those of the independent teacher. The things described above (and other similar happenings) are certainly not conducive to promoting the aura of professionalism which should be an important goal for each of us. Not only must we establish appropriate standards, but we must also maintain them — not just in our teaching, but also in every other aspect of our professional undertakings.

13

Miscellaneous Studio Events and Procedures

▶ ANNUAL PARENTS' MEETINGS

In the institutional preparatory departments with which I was involved, we had a parents' meeting at the start of each new academic year. We always scheduled it to occur on two different evenings so that those who could not attend on one night could come on the other. At the meeting, the director of the department first presented a brief general discussion of the purpose and goals of the curriculum, as well as a review of the practice requirements and some of the other items contained in the department's policy statement. Following this, the parents met in small groups with their own child's teacher and participated in informal discussions of the goals and expectations for the coming year of study.

Whenever I had students in a home studio, I also scheduled similar meetings for the parents of those students as well. Sometimes it was a morning brunch, or sometimes an evening dessert and coffee. Such events in both the institutions and the home studio were always very well attended and I believe did much to facilitate a smooth and enthusiastic start to a new teaching year.

▶ PARENT VISITS TO LESSONS

I require that parents attend *all* lessons of children under the age of eight. Parents of all other students are encouraged to attend lessons whenever they wish, but I do ask to always be informed of their intention to do this prior to the actual day of the lesson.

I think that it is a good idea for a parent to visit a few lessons early in the new teaching year in order to be able to observe the practice procedures that are being emphasized. (This is especially useful for the parents of beginners and new transfer students.) When parents do attend the lesson, they understand that they are not to interject comments to either me or the student during the course of the lesson. Although I may sometimes choose to direct certain remarks or questions to them, they are otherwise requested to remain silent.

Some parents want to attend all of their child's lessons for as long as he/she studies. Most of the time, this is fine; however, upon occasion, I have decided that I would like to have the opportunity of working with a particular student *without* an auditing parent present. More often than not, we discover that many students become entirely different people when a parent is not looking on. Should I decide that this *modus operandi* is in the best interest of the student, I discuss my reasons for this decision with the parent and request that we suspend parent visits until further notice. (When this occurs, I remind parents that they can always review the audio or video recording that is made at each lesson in order to find out what transpired.)

I think that inviting parents to attend at least one lesson per term is a good idea. I usually schedule these visits at the end of a term and among other things, the student plans a special "recital" to display some of the things that he or she has accomplished during the term.

▶ THE WEEKLY ASSIGNMENT SHEET

In addition to having either an audio or video recording for reference, I think that it is also important for students to receive a *written* weekly assignment sheet to serve as a general guide for the coming week of practice. I provide my students with a two-page pre-printed sheet, shown on the following pages, which is 3-hole punched and then placed in the student's binder notebook at the end of each lesson. During the lesson, I make a copy of whatever I write on the sheet so that I always know exactly what has been assigned. I also use this copy as an aid to planning the following week's lesson.

ASSIGNMENT SHEET (page 1)

Assignment Sheet for: _____
(Name of Student)

Quarter:_____   Lesson #:_____   Date: _____

REMINDERS:
    1) Group Lesson Date:_____   Time:_____
       Performance pieces: _____
    2) Memory Piece(s): _____
    3) Creative Piece Plan: _____
    4) Your choice for next week's "Begin-the-Lesson" Piece: _____

For each category below, put a ✓ in the left-hand column beside each activity every time you do it.
Also be sure to answer the questions at the bottom of page 2.

About keeping your daily practice record: On page 2, write down the total of each day's practice time.
Be sure that a parent signs the record before you return for your next lesson.

===

MARK ✓'s in the left hand column below every time you do the activity or piece.

TECHNIQUE WARM-UPS   **GOALS**

_____   1) _____ Create your own warm-up.   MM= _____

_____   2) **Syllabus**, pp. _____, Ex. # _____ MM= _____
                              Keys: _____HS 1st_____ then HT _____

_____   3) **Scales:** Keys _____
                              MM= _____ HS 1st _____ then HT _____

Practice suggestions: _____
_____

                              4) **Arpeggios:** Keys _____
                              MM= _____ HS 1st _____ then HT _____

Practice suggestions: _____
_____

                              5) **Other** _____

===

THEORY   **GOALS**
_____   **Syllabus**, pp. _____, Ex. # _____
                          Keys: _____

Practice suggestions: _____
_____

ASSIGNMENT SHEET (page 2)

REVIEW PIECES

Repertiore   **GOALS/Practice Steps**

_____ pp._____   _____
_____ pp._____   _____
_____ pp._____   _____
_____ pp._____   _____
_____ pp._____   _____
_____ pp._____   _____
_____ pp._____   _____

==

NEW PIECES

Repertiore   **GOALS/Practice Steps**

_____ pp._____   _____
_____ pp._____   _____
_____ pp._____   _____
_____ pp._____   _____
_____ Sight-Playing pp. _____

==

PRACTICE RECORD

Mon	Tues	Wed	Thu	Fri	Sat	Sun

This week's average: _____minutes

Signature of Parent: _____

Questions about this week's practice:

    With which piece did you make the most progress?_____

    What was your favorite piece?_____

    Your least favorite piece? _____

    What new words did you look up in your music dictionary? _____

    _____

    (Did you write their definition in your music? _____ Yes _____ No)

    Have you numbered all the measures in your pieces? _____ Yes _____ No

    On a scale of 1 to 10 (with 10 as highest), rate this week's practice: _____

Other messages/reminders:

PRACTICE RECORDS

Throughout the school year, my students are asked to record their daily practice time on a practice record that appears right on each weekly assignment sheet. (This can be seen on page 2 of the assignment sheet.) Prior to each lesson, a parent is asked to sign the record. This at least encourages a parent to get some idea of when and for how long the student says she is spending at the piano every day.

At each lesson, the first thing we do is average the week's daily practice minutes. (Since I only require that a student practice *five* days a week, I divide the total accumulated minutes by five.) We then record the week's average on the studio's ongoing practice chart. At the end of a term when I send home a progress report to parents, I always include the student's overall average daily practice time, comparing it to the *expected* amount of time that was agreed upon at the start of the year.

Even though the primary emphasis in practice is always on *how* the student practices and on *mind spent* as opposed to just *time spent*, how long a student practices and the regularity of its occurrence does, without a doubt, affect his accomplishment. It also provides a *specific* measurement which both the student and parent can actually see. For instance, if lack of progress is an issue, it is sometimes easier for them to relate this to inadequate and inconsistent practice than to the pedagogical considerations which define effective practice.

 STUDENT PROGRESS REPORTS

I send out two progress reports during the academic year – one at the end of the first 12-week term, and then one at the end of the spring term. Below is a sample of what is included in these reports.

From the Studio of Elvina Truman Pearce

Progress Report for: *Jason Scott*

Fall/Winter, 2014-15   Date: December 28, 2014

Practice
Recommended daily practice average for students in grades 6-8: 45 minutes (based on a 5-day week).
Jason's daily average (based on 10 recorded weeks) is: 47 minutes

I am pleased that Jason's average continues to be at least 45 minutes per day. (I continue to emphasize that this average should be for a 5-day week as opposed to practicing longer on just 2-3 days because it is the *daily* reinforcement that plays a significant role in the formation of habits – especially physical habits related to technical proficiency. Better to practice a bit less each day for 5 days than to try to cram it all into 2-3 days.)

About following the assignment and weekly preparation

At the beginning of the term, Jason's weekly preparation was less satisfactory than it was for most of last year. For just one example, he was very careless with fingering. When I finally told him that I would no longer hear any pieces that reflected less than accurate fingering, he shaped up rather quickly, and, since then, he seems to be back on track with this. I've found that carelessness with fingering as well as with other things related to careful preparation of the weekly assignment seems to be rather common with students of junior high age, and we must "nip" such things "in the bud" or else they can really inhibit the student's overall success and progress.

I do think that Jason makes an effort to utilize the practice steps that we do at the lesson and which are assigned for home practice. Hopefully, his reviewing of the video made at each lesson will be a useful guide for effective practice — particularly during the first few days after the lesson. He now seems to be much more aware of the importance of applying practice strategies such as *slow* practice, hands separate practice, counting aloud, etc., than he was last year. And as he becomes more and more aware that these procedures actually *reduce* the amount of time it takes to learn a new piece as well as guarantee success, he will be much more willing to utilize them in his practice.

About technique

Jason's scale and arpeggio playing are both progressing well. He still needs to monitor the positioning of his thumbs, along with the height of his wrists. When he thinks of these things as he plays slowly and hands separately, it makes a big difference, and will little by little become an integral part of his technical approach to the piano. I also believe that his sitting posture at the instrument is improving, although occasionally I still need to remind him not to "slump" and to be sure that his two feet are positioned flat on the floor unless he is using the pedal. Overall, however, I am pleased with his technical development.

Musical expression

Jason continues to be a very expressive player. He understands musical goals and he really *listens* to himself when he plays. As a performer, he gets very involved in re-creating the musical messages which he thinks the composer wants to communicate. He does a good job with producing dynamic contrasts, and he has a natural sense of timing and artistic phrasing. He is also becoming much more able to control and maintain an established tempo without rushing or slowing down in the hard spots. I believe that he truly loves music and making it at the piano, and we must be sure that this continues!

Student's attitude

Jason continues to have a very good attitude at his lessons. He is pleasant and cooperative and really tries to do everything he is asked to do. I think that for the most part he enjoys his lessons. I trust that if you ever sense any major changes in his attitude about either lessons or practicing which persist over an extended period of time, you will advise me of this, and, of course, I'll communicate any concerns that I might have along these lines to you should they occur. Right now, everything seems fine and we want to keep it that way!

Miscellaneous comments

I am happy that Jason entered the sonata/sonatina festival and that he did so well. I was also extremely pleased with his performances at the December recital. I am planning for him to enter another competition in April (to be preceded by a performance in one of our music teacher organization's student recitals in February). These two events will give him two additional specific goals and I think will be good for him both psychologically and musically. I'll give you more information about these performance events as soon as the details have been confirmed.

As always, your interest and support of Jason's musical endeavors is very important, and I appreciate it! Thank you.

P.S. Because of the level of music he is now working on, Jason needs to have access to a music dictionary. Can you please purchase one for him? (You can buy an inexpensive small paperback dictionary at any music store, and he should keep it at the piano with his music and also bring it to his lessons.)

I have found that parents are very appreciative of regular reports such as the above about their child's progress and they frequently respond via a phone call or an email message. Although it takes a considerable amount of time to prepare each report, in my opinion, it is well worth the time and effort.

▶ USE OF RECORDING DEVICES AT THE LESSON

For years, an audio cassette recorder was a standard part of my studio equipment and each student was asked to bring a blank cassette tape to every lesson. Since students now have access to various technologies for recording, students can easily make an audio or even video recording of the lesson. In either the audio or video format, we record whatever portions of the lesson which I think will provide significant guidelines for the coming week of practice.

Another real advantage of recording practice suggestions is that it eliminates the need for the teacher to do so much writing on the assignment sheet during the lesson. Since we can talk through and record practice procedures in "real time" as the student is actually doing them, this does not take any additional lesson time as does having to stop to write out all of this information. On the assignment sheet, I always write "√ R" beside the listing of all pieces and/or activities that have been dealt with and recorded at the lesson and this alerts students to check this recording as they practice.

It is always quite obvious which students have actually referred to the recording as preparation for their next lesson. Over the years, I have found that those students who consistently utilize the recording are usually better prepared for the next lesson than those who don't. I also encourage parents to listen to (or view) the recordings so that they can have a better idea of what their child is supposed to be doing when practicing rather than just sitting at the piano and playing through the pieces on the assignment.

PART THREE:
FINALE

A Forum for Miscellaneous Questions and Answers

Since the late 1950s, I have been involved in teachers' workshops, both as an attendee and as a presenter, and, over the course of those many years, one of the things I have always found most stimulating and interesting are the questions that are raised and discussed by the teachers in attendance. I find that most of these same issues continue to surface at 21st century workshops and this only confirms my belief that many of our own problems and concerns related to piano teaching are universally shared by *all* piano teachers — and especially by those of us who work with traditional ("average") boys and girls in their pre-college years. This final chapter presents a compilation of some of the issues about which teachers seem to have the most concern, and, in response, I shall share a few ideas about ways we might deal with them.

(I was recently asked to speak at an annual seminar attended by the faculty of an area community music school, and it was requested that I address the first two questions that follow. The answers here are actual excerpts from the lecture that I presented at that event.)

Q: How can we maintain a high standard of music education in our current culture when the trend seems to be to expose children to as many different activities as possible?

A: Well, first of all, so long as parents go along with such a trend, we obviously can't do anything to change their willingness to allow their children to take part in as many extra-curricular activities as are humanly possible. The only thing we can do is to decide how we are going to deal with this situation. For me, this is a no-brainer. Although I obviously can't control anything that goes on outside of my studio, I most surely can control 100% of what happens therein. I have just one option and it is to continue to maintain only the highest standards in music education, to remain firm about upholding these standards, and to never lower my expectations for student achievement, regardless of how many other activities the student may be involved with.

Q: *But how can we remain firm about not lowering our standards and expectations and still keep students enrolled in our studio classes – especially if our demands seem so much higher than those which the students are accustomed to in so many of their other activities – both in and outside of school?*

A: As I see it, the answer is two-fold. First of all, I truly believe that we maintain music students not by *lowering* our standards, but rather, by *raising* the students' awareness of the joy inherent in the world of music itself. And secondly, once students are turned on to "good" music, I believe that we can maintain our studio enrollment by making sure that our students are acquiring the reading, technical, and practice skills necessary for being able to successfully make music *themselves.*

In my own teaching career, I have rarely lost students who played so well that they were able to truly love the experience of making music at the piano. Here, I think that the key word is LOVE. "I love playing the piano because I love music itself! I love the pieces my teacher assigns! I love playing because I like what I hear when I play, and I also love playing because it's something that I've learned how to do successfully all by myself."

Rather than lamenting the over-scheduling of today's students or the seeming lack of high standards and expectations of excellence in other areas; rather than harboring the fear that we shall lose students unless we do indeed lower our own standards and expectations for their musical growth, I think we need to be focusing on the *success factor — and how to achieve it with every single student at every single lesson.* One way to do this is to be sure that each lesson is a special event which provides students with many rewarding musical experiences and provides the acquisition of the tools needed in order to become musically literate and physically adept at expressing what they understand within a musical context.

Q: *Some teachers refrain from playing their student's pieces for them because they are afraid that the students will imitate them. What is your opinion about this?*

A: It is my belief that many teachers need to do a lot more modeling for their students. *How can we expect students to become enthusiastic about learning to play a piece when they have no idea what it sounds like??* And if students don't hear their pieces played superbly at their lessons, when and where will they hear them?

The subject of "modeling" always reminds me of an event from my past that occurred at a 1960s meeting of our local music teachers' association. The guest speaker was a woman who was, by reputation, a fine teacher as well as a first-rate musician and pianist. Although I don't remember the subject of her presentation on that day, I do recall one statement that she made. In essence, she said very emphatically: *"I never play for my students because I don't want them to imitate me."*

All I could think of then — and still today, some 40 years later — is *why should being able to imitate such beautiful music-making be undesirable?* I would submit that if more students were able to play as beautifully and effortlessly as did this woman, the drop-out rate in studios would be drastically reduced.

Relative to this, I've made a checklist of questions which we as teachers might ask ourselves at the end of each teaching day.

End of the Teaching Day — Question #1

In all of today's lessons, did *every* student have an opportunity to hear at least *some* "good" music performed "live" and *really* well — with artistry, authority, enthusiasm, energy, vitality, drama, and imagination? And was it obvious to the student that the performer was truly *enjoying* the performance experience?

End of the Teaching Day — Question #2

In every lesson today, did each student have an opportunity to play at least one piece — a favorite which she really likes and can play at a reasonable tempo and with an acceptable degree of accuracy and technical security and after which the teacher can honestly say, "Good job!", or "That was really exciting!", or "What fun!", or "What a beautiful mood you created with that performance!" etc.

Apropos of this, in one of my student's lessons right before Christmas, we ended the lesson by playing the Dello Joio duet arrangement of "Silent Night" from his *Christmas Music* (EB Marks/Hal Leonard). The student, an 11-year-old girl, played the piece so expressively and with such obvious love that, at the end of our performance, I said, "How wonderful you must feel about being able to play so beautifully." And when I looked at her face, it was just glowing! The question is: *Do all of our students have this kind of a "glowing" experience at least once at every lesson with music which they themselves make?*

As a sidebar, let me add a couple of other thoughts. I believe that sub-standard performances and the lack of physical ease and enjoyment when playing are frequently the result of students being assigned music that is beyond them — not only technically, but also emotionally and intellectually. I also believe that many students discontinue music lessons not so much because of their preference for or over-involvement in other activities, but because when they play, they just don't sound good enough to like what they hear, and they don't know what to do about it. Hence, much of what they play remains pretty unrewarding. Of course, poor practice habits also contribute to unrewarding performances (and frequently to drop-outs), and so the subject of practice generates two more important questions for our end-of-the-day checklist:

End of the Teaching Day — Question #3

Did every student leave today's lesson being aware of the success they experienced when they used specific practice techniques that enabled them to achieve more accuracy and technical security, either in problem spots in a piece-in-progress, or as an aid to working out a brand new piece?

End of the Teaching Day — Question #4

Did every student leave today's lesson with specific guidelines for the coming week of home practice so that they know *exactly* what their goals are for each piece and activity on the assignment sheet as well as specifically what to do to achieve them?

Q: You have spoken a lot about the importance of students having regular group lesson experiences. Could you elaborate on the equipment needed for group lessons and also on some of the specific activities that the students do in these classes?

A: Your question about the equipment needed for group lessons is an easy one to answer. *All that is needed is one piano and two or more students* — plus an enthusiastic and well-organized teacher! For younger, early-level students, I do think it's essential to also have a dry marker board, some plastic or cardboard "dummy" keyboards, and some flash cards. (All of my cards are homemade with a magic marker on letter-sized biology filler paper.)

Before discussing group lesson activities, I want to say a bit about group lessons in general. I have been working with students in groups since the late 1950s, and, over these many years, I have come to believe that group experiences are not only a *plus* for the private student, but that they are actually a *necessity*. For this reason, I enroll no students on a private-only basis. Instead, my study plan always includes both a weekly individual lesson and a once-a-month group lesson. During group lesson weeks, the private lesson is abbreviated — 45-minute lessons become 30-minute lessons, and one-hour lessons become 45-minute lessons. This abbreviation procedure frees up enough time in my schedule to make it possible for me to add the class lessons.

As I see it, the primary goal of group lessons is to provide students with regular performance opportunities which enable them to share music and what they are learning about it with others — specifically, with their peers.

I group students according to their age and grade in school, and I think that the ideal number of students in a group is four. In most of my classes, there are three or four students and the group meets for one hour each month. Sometimes the group lessons of older and more advanced students will last for an hour and a half. Occasionally there will be only two students in a group (in which case we call it a "partner" lesson). In partner lessons, we overlap the lessons of the two students whose individual lessons are scheduled back-to-back and midway between their two private lessons, they meet together for a partner lesson lasting for 30-45 minutes, depending upon the age and performance level of the students.

At each class, every student always performs a minimum of two or three pieces — one being a memory piece. In addition, each student also performs a creative piece of his own making based on compositional criteria presented at the previous month's group lesson.

Group Lesson Activities

We generally begin the class with some sort of a technical warm-up. For this activity, each student may do a brief individual warm-up, or sometimes two students will warm-up together, playing a dictated, easy-to-remember 5-finger pattern of some sort. (If there are two pianos in a studio, four students can occasionally do their warm-up together.) Once in a while, the students themselves create the warm-up patterns. Sometimes the warm-up might be a scale or an arpeggio from their current assignment. During the warm-ups, those who are not warming up always serve as "monitors" who are asked to check things such as the players' hand positions (the arch, the placement of the fingers on the keys, the wrist, etc.). They also check the players' posture, the placement of their feet, the quality of their tone (Is it clear, well projected, and "singing?"), etc.

After the warm-up, we usually hear each student play a piece. Of course, having a ready-made audience for which to perform on a regular basis is wonderful! But besides providing students with regular performance opportunities, group lessons also provide them with opportunities to become active as *listeners* — not only to their own performance but also to the performances of others. An important challenge for the teacher is to be sure that each *non-performer* is always as actively involved with *listening* as is the student who is performing at the piano. (Usually there is more than one copy of the music available so that students can follow the score as they listen. If not, then they are asked to gather around the piano and look at the music on the rack as it is being played.)

Here are some ways to involve students in active listening:

- Assign each *non-performer* one specific thing to listen for as she follows the score while listening to the performance. (For example, one student might be asked to listen specifically for the dynamics changes, another student would check on the *legato* and *staccatos*, still another might be asked to check on *fermatas*, *ritards*, or *accelerandos*, or phrase endings, or for clarity in pedal changes, etc.).

  At the end of the performance, each *non-performing* student is then asked to report on the performer's success in projecting the specific thing(s) that the auditor was asked to listen for.

- Ask each *non-performer* to examine the score and select two specific things to listen for but to *not tell* the other students what they are. At the end of the performance, each student reveals the two things he chose to listen for, and then is asked to evaluate the performer's success in projecting them.

- Prior to hearing a performance, tell the *non-performers* that at the end of it, they will be asked to mention one thing that they thought the performer did very well, and one thing that might be added or changed to make the playing even more effective.

- Ask the *non-performers* to serve as "judges" and rate each performance on a scale of one to ten. As they listen, the "judges" are asked to list on paper all of the good things about the performance as well as those things which the student might do to enhance it. At the end of each performance, the teacher averages the numerical scores, announces the performer's overall score, and then reads aloud the "judges" comments (without identifying who said what).

(This activity is particularly effective for older and more advanced students who are in the process of preparing to enter an audition or contest.)

The teacher may also sometimes suggest listening activities to be done *without* the auditors seeing the score first, and without following the music as it is being performed. For example:

- As they listen to a performance, ask the *non-performers* to make a list of all symbols which describe things that they heard (*f*, *p*, slurs, *staccato*, *fermata*, pedal, etc.). It is always fun to compare lists and to see who ends up with the longest one!

- Strictly on the basis of listening, ask students to determine a piece's *form*, or its *quality* (major or minor?), or to describe its *character* (mood), etc.

Of course during each of the performance segments, there is always some critiquing. Ideally, most of the comments and suggestions will come from the students themselves rather than from the teacher. In my own group lessons, I view my role as primarily that of a facilitator whose job is:

1. to plan and steer the content and form of the class, and
2. to be sure that the lesson environment remains positive so that each student can feel comfortable and experience both success and the genuine enjoyment that should be the result of music-making at the piano.

Besides performance, we also usually include a few brief drills in the areas of reading, rhythm, aural awareness, and theory. These drills are interspersed between performance segments to provide a change of pace as well as to assist with reinforcing whatever concepts the students are in the process of learning. However, because the major emphasis of every class is always on making and listening to music, we never spend more than a total of 10-15 minutes in any one-hour class on drills.

Q: *How do you get students involved with composing their own pieces?*

A: One of the best ways I've found to do this is to assign all students to create a piece of their own to perform at every monthly group lesson. The subject and/or structural format for the creative piece is always assigned and illustrated at the preceding month's group lesson. Because of the restrictions imposed by having to notate these pieces, particularly at the earlier levels, the students are not required to write them out – only to remember them so that they can play them securely and convincingly for the class.

Q: *What are some of the reasons why we should emphasize student composing?*

A: Why should teachers make room for composing in their already jammed lesson agendas? The first reason that occurs to me is that composing is just plain fun! We know that all students love to doodle at the piano, and they probably loved doing this *long before* they ever were enrolled for a piano lesson. This enjoyment of doodling and experimenting with sounds at the keyboard is a characteristic that I believe should be nurtured and enlarged upon rather than ignored or, worse yet, discouraged. We all stress working at the piano, but I wonder if we place equal emphasis on maintaining the "*play*" aspect of music-making. Emphasizing student composing is one very good way to do this.

A second reason for student composing is that it involves the imagination, and this inevitably spills over into the student's approach to performing the music of others. Students who must draw upon their own imaginations to make pieces of their own will learn more quickly that music is a communicative art whose purpose is to express various ideas and feelings. This concept certainly affects their approach when they perform the music of others.

A third reason for making creative assignments is that composing provides a great way to reinforce all of the concepts being presented in the coursework. For example, if a young student is learning about *staccato* and *legato*, making her own pieces using these two elements will really underline their meaning and make the student more aware of hearing and executing them when they are found in the music of other composers.

Q: Can I teach composing even though I, myself, don't compose?

A: Absolutely! But I also think that you can compose! I truly believe that anyone of us with an imagination, a fairly well-developed sense of musicality, and a good working knowledge of the keyboard can learn to compose and to do it *well*. All it takes are two things: first, having an idea for a subject and structural format, and second, spending some time "doodling" – experimenting at the keyboard.

For example, suppose we were given the assignment of making an elementary-level piece about "Chimes." In it, we are told to choose just *one* blocked 5th to use in the *LH* and the notes of *one* Major 5-finger pattern in the *RH*, and to include the use of the pedal. Experimenting and doodling around a bit with these elements, I'm sure that every one of us could make a piece that would sound like the ringing of chimes.

Or perhaps our assignment might be to make a piece about corn popping. In it we are told to use *staccatos* and only the five black keys. Once again experimenting a bit at the piano with these specifications, it would be fairly easy to come up with a piece that could describe corn popping.

Q: When should student composing begin?

A: My answer to this question is "At once! Right from the very first lesson." And this is possible regardless of the age of the student or what course or method is being used.

My beginners start out by using an all-black key format for their creative pieces, and they are always given a few ideas for what a piece might be about (a frog jumping, an elevator, rain falling, etc.) Every beginner (either a child or an adult) can, *without reading*, make some very effective pieces using just the above as guidelines.

Now obviously at this point, beginners can't notate their pieces and I *don't want them to!* Why? Because if notation is one of the criteria for composing at this level, then the student is severely limited to only what he is able to read and/or write. Instead of imposing restrictions on their creativity, I want to encourage them to experience complete freedom at the keyboard, *e.g.*, making pieces that use the *whole* keyboard, playing with *both* hands, using all levels of loud's and soft's, using *staccatos* and *legato*, using pedal, etc.

My only stipulation for student composing is that they are able to recall their pieces and to repeat them in their *exact* form numerous times if asked to do so. (Students soon learn that this usually means making a short piece so that it is easy to remember.)

Q: *What are some of the ideas you might suggest as the basis for creative pieces?*

A: In my studio, the student is *always* given specific guidelines for the structure of every creative piece. This is different from my simply saying, "For next month's group lesson, make up a piece of your own." Were I to give this type of a broad, open-ended assignment, there would be so many options to consider that, more than likely, many students would return saying, "I couldn't think of anything to make a piece about." So, to avoid this, I always provide some very *specific* structural guidelines and illustrate at the keyboard several ways that students might use these in creating their own pieces. Although all of the students in the group use the *same* structural idea as the basis for their compositions, of course no two pieces are ever alike, and it is always great fun to hear the variety that occurs.

Here is a list of eighteen different ideas for creative piece assignments.

Ideas for Creative Piece Assignments

- Make a piece using only *black* keys.

- Make a piece using only *black* keys in one hand and only *white* keys in the other.

- With one hand, play only 5ths (either blocked or broken), and, with the other hand, play just *one* other interval. (It could be only 3rds, or only 4ths, etc.)

- Make a piece accompanied by a single *ostinato* pattern. (The *ostinato* could occur in the *LH* or it could be in the *RH*.)

- Make a piece using either A-B-A or A-B-A¹ form.

- Make an A-B-A piece in which the A part is *major* and B part is *minor*.

- Make a piece that contains augmented and/or diminished triads (either blocked or broken).

- Make a piece that contains both triads and inversions (either major or minor).

- Create several variations for a familiar tune (such as "Twinkle," "Go Tell Aunt Rhody," the Pachelbel Canon, etc.).

- Create a new B part for an A-B-A piece. *For this assignment, I give students a short easy piece with A-B-A structure which they can practically sight-read. For the next class, they will each play the piece as it is written, and then play it once more but this time substituting their own B part for the original one.*

- Learn a short segment of a piece (4 measures) and create an ending for it. *Here again, I give them a copy of a simple 4-measure segment.*

- Make a piece that uses hand-over-hand crossovers and pedal.

- Make a piece that uses both *consonant* and *dissonant* intervals.

- Make a bitonal piece (with one hand playing in a major key and the other in minor, or a piece that uses a different major key in each hand, etc.).

- Improvise on a *blues* pattern (a 12-bar blues).

- Set a story (or parts of a story) to music. *For this, I would have the students agree on what the story is to be about.*

- Make a piece that characterizes one particular mood or condition — happy, sad, sleepy, scared, etc. *In this case, ask each student to choose the mood he/she wants to express, and then see if the other class members can guess what it is when they hear the piece at next month's class.*

- Write different subject titles on separate slips of paper and have students pick one at random. Their next creative piece will describe whatever subject was suggested on the slip of paper they drew.

In summary

Without a doubt, students thoroughly enjoy making pieces of their own and are very good at it provided they are given adequate guidelines for structuring them. As teachers, I think it's important that for the creative assignment, we don't try to impose our own ideas upon students or suggest changes that we think would improve their pieces. I think that a better approach is simply to stand back and admire whatever the students come up with, and to continue to encourage them to explore all of the possibilities which their own imaginations might suggest.

Surely one of the best ways to become musically literate is to make the musical language our own by using it to organize and communicate our *own* ideas instead of only just reproducing the musical ideas of others. Composing adds this important dimension to the musical education of our students, and having an opportunity to share their creativity with their peers at each group lesson (or in a recital) provides a great incentive for composing.

Q: What is the difference between "coaching" and "teaching?"

A: The difference between these two teaching approaches is hard to define, and there is usually always some overlap from one to the other. When dealing with the performance of a piece of music, I think of "coaching" as a teacher's telling a student what to do in that specific piece, *e.g.*, "Play loudly here"; "Broaden this *ritard* a bit more"; "Change the pedal on counts one and three"; "Add a bit of a *crescendo* here"; "Play the *LH* part softer than the *RH.*" "Coaching" is the approach which is generally used by artist teachers when working with students in a master class situation. Although the student's performance of the piece may significantly improve as the result of what the teacher tells her to do, are the reasons for the teacher's conclusions understood? And how much of this information will spill over and be useful to the student in other repertoire she is currently working on or may work on in the future?

In the area of performance, I think that "teaching" differs from "coaching" in that the teacher leads the student to make interpretive changes based on discovering a *reason* for them, *e.g.*, "Why play louder here?"; "Why might a *crescendo* be appropriate at this point?"; "Why play the *LH* softer than the *RH* in this segment?" In this approach, the big issue is not so much on *what* to do, but rather on *why* suggested changes are appropriate. One excellent way for the teacher to assist the student in discovering an appropriate answer is to play a passage two ways and then ask the student which way she prefers and why?

To summarize — in "coaching" the emphasis is primarily on *what* to do; in "teaching" the emphasis is on the student's gaining an understanding of *why* to do it. In my opinion, the ongoing concern of the teacher always needs to be on ensuring the student's ability to apply what is said and done at the lesson to subsequent musical situations. Of course it's up to the teacher to determine when either "coaching" or "teaching" is appropriate, and to be sure that there is always a healthy balance maintained between the two.

Q: *How long are your students' lessons?*

A: This is a question that I am frequently asked when I do a teachers' workshop. About one-third of my studio is enrolled for one-hour weekly private lessons and the rest of them have 45-minute lessons. (In addition, they all have a group lesson once a month for which there is no extra charge.)

A good many years ago I came to the conclusion that it was totally impossible in a once-a-week, 30-minute private lesson to be able to provide my students with the kind of musical and pianistic education I felt was imperative. Consequently, I decided to no longer offer 30-minute lessons as an option. I have often heard discussions of this issue among my colleagues, and it is not at all uncommon to hear expressions of concern about the possibility of losing half of their class of students were they to eliminate 30-minute lessons. This has certainly not been the case in my studio, and I would urge teachers who yearn for more time with their students to be willing to "live dangerously" and give it a try. If one doesn't want to impose this lesson-length change for current students, perhaps one might instead consider making it effective for all new students being added to the roster.

Q: *What do you do with students who are oblivious to fingering and the role it plays in successfully learning new pieces?*

A: This is rarely a problem with beginners who, from the very first lesson, are made aware that observing the fingering is always just as important as playing the correct notes, the correct rhythm, etc. In my experience, most of the students who seem to be "oblivious" to fingering are usually transfer students, and, because they have been overlooking fingering for a considerable length of time, it's a hard habit to break. Here are three procedures I have used for dealing with the fingering dilemma:

1. Whenever a student plays an incorrect finger, the *student* — NOT the *teacher* — writes in the *correct* finger number and circles it in red. (I am 100% positive that students will always pay more attention to the things *they* write than to anything the teacher might write.)

2. I sometimes ask a student who is careless about fingering to write onto the score of every new piece the finger number for each note *before* beginning to practice it. (This is assuming, of course, that the student is not a beginner and is already a fairly decent note reader who will not be reading the piece by finger numbers.) As stated above, my belief is that students will be much more apt to observe the fingering that *they*, themselves, create rather than observe that which the composer or editor has already indicated in the printedscore, or which the teacher writes in for them.

3. Each week, give the student a copy of part of a piece which has *no* fingering at all. This should be a piece that is considerably easier than the student's regular repertoire. It is usually necessary to white-out any existing finger numbers in the piece and then photocopy it for the student. (Duplication of music being used for educational purposes is permissible so long as it is done from a *purchased* copy and is of only a *small* part of a composition. Such photocopies should be destroyed after the student has used them.)

Ask the student to write in the fingering on the photocopy and then plan to play it at the next lesson using his fingering. At that time, praise the student for all wise choices that were made. If, in some spots, there are better fingering possibilities, discuss the reasons for preferring them. Then reassign the piece so that the student can have an opportunity to try the fingering changes that were agreed upon at this week's lesson.

Q: *What do you do with students who refuse to count aloud?*

A: First of all, counting aloud is *not* optional for beginning students. Because, from the very start, it has been a part of the student's practice strategies for learning each new piece, it soon becomes a part of her habit and therefore it seldom becomes an issue.

As soon as I'm sure that a student has mastered the art of simultaneously playing and counting aloud (usually after about a year or so of lessons), I no longer require that he count aloud at the lesson unless he is playing an incorrect rhythm. Whenever this happens, then the student knows that he will be asked to play and count *aloud*. If a student's tendency is to count so softly that I can barely hear it, I will position myself across the room and insist that the counting be loud enough for me to easily hear it from this location.

Undoubtedly there are numerous ways to get students to count aloud as they play, but rather than discussing these, I would like to focus instead on one way that for sure *won't* accomplish this and that's for the teacher to count *with* them. As I think about solving this "no-counting-aloud" problem, I always think about Bobby, a former student in my early years of teaching. Bobby absolutely *refused* to count. I tried everything I could think of to rectify this situation. At every lesson, I would shout "Count!" before he started each piece. Then he would begin to play, but only *I* counted. Regardless of how loudly I counted, Bobby *never* counted along with me. Finally, one day I became acutely aware that the only voice I ever heard counting in that studio was *mine*. (And not just with Bobby but with other students as well.) From that day on, I vowed to break my habit of counting aloud with my students, and I did. Although now I sometimes count along with them at the outset of a lesson performance just to get the music in motion, I withdraw almost at once, and then the ball is in their court.

Why should students count if someone else always does it for them? If we expect them to count by themselves at home when they practice, then they must surely be able to do so at the lesson.

Q: *You have not addressed the subject of the use of technology in the piano studio. What do you use in addition to the piano?*

A: I do not use technology as a teaching tool – unless you consider an audio or video recorder and a dry marker board as components of "technology." Nor do I enroll any student who does not have access to an acoustic piano on which to practice. A number of my students have digital keyboards and other technological accessories which they enjoy using, and I am 100% supportive of this. However, I believe that there is a vast difference between creating music "from scratch" on an acoustic piano and creating it on a digital instrument, and this is why I require that my students' piano practice be done on the former. Surely the 21st century's "computerization" of today's young people provides them with abundant experience utilizing technology, and this is important. But I contend that it is equally important for them to also be able to "click themselves on" and learn how to function and be creative on their own *without* relying on the use of technology. *Enter the acoustic piano!*

Q: *What are your most important priorities in student/teacher relationships?*

A: I think that whenever teachers pursue a topic such as this, the discussion is usually approached from the point of view of the teachers – "What can we, as teachers, do to develop and sustain positive, productive relationships with our students?"

But there's another approach to discussing a subject such as this and that is to examine it from the *student*'s perspective rather than from our own. This is the view I decided to take in this discussion, and as preparation, I took a nostalgic journey back through my own student days. Starting with grade one and proceeding upward to my post-college years, I made a list of all of the teachers with whom I thought that I, as a student, had had a significant relationship. The list turned out to be very short — actually only five teachers made the final cut.

These five relationships were not necessarily all close, personal, or long-term, but nonetheless they are all memorable because they helped to shape not only my career but also my life, contributing significantly to who and what I am today.

An interesting exercise might be for each of *you* to make a similar list of the teachers who actually had a major impact on *your* life. Were you to do this, I would guess that your lists would also be short, probably ending up with not more than a half dozen individuals. A second interesting exercise for you would be to try to determine just what it was that made each of these relationships important enough for you to remember. I think that this points up the fact that meaningful student/teacher relationships are not everyday occurrences. But those teachers that we do remember are the ones who surely must have succeeded in developing *significant* relationships with us or else we wouldn't have remembered them.

Jane Harnish
(my first-grade teacher)

I can certainly tell you why I remember Jane Harnish — the first teacher on my list. Miss Harnish was my first-grade teacher, a no-nonsense kind of person who, to us six-year-olds, seemed to be at least 100 years old and 7 feet tall. Actually, she was sort of a senior citizen version of Popeye's Olive Oyl with her grey hair fastened in a knot at the nape of her neck, and wearing thick-lens glasses, tweedy clothes, and big brown oxfords. (When we were not in her presence, we often referred to her as "Old Harny Toad.") Suffice it to say that just *looking* at Jane Harnish was enough to make most six-year-olds remember her!

But regardless of her looks, as soon as we entered her classroom, the magic began! I'm positive that Miss Harnish was the originator of the "Hooked on Phonics" approach to reading and boy, did we phonate! Needless to say, because of this, we did *indeed* learn how to read and spell. In addition, she also taught us how to write, and, as she walked from desk to desk peering over our shoulders, she made it perfectly clear that anything less than 100% neatness and legibility was totally unacceptable.

I don't remember ever having "fun" in Jane Harnish's class — at least not "fun" as beheld through the eyes of a 6-year-old — but I *do* remember the aura of adventure that permeated that room because learning was always taking place there. As a matter of fact, I believe that my first awareness of the joy of learning was actually born right there in Room One. My student/teacher relationship with Jane Harnish, although lasting but a year, remains meaningful to this day, not because she was pretty, or witty, or nice, or fun, but because she was determined that every single pupil in that class would leave the first grade soundly grounded in the basics necessary for literacy, and we did! I remember that she expected — in fact, *demanded* — great things of us, and as a result, we succeeded! Although I didn't know it at age six, I now know that it was our *success* that was to make this student/teacher relationship significant and memorable.

I have just described how I, as a *student*, remember my relationship with Jane Harnish. As a teacher, although I would of course love being remembered by my students as being pretty, witty, nice, and fun, I would much prefer being remembered as one who, like Miss Harnish, was determined that my students become musically literate and able to sound good when they play the piano; and I would also like to be remembered as one who always expected and demanded great things of them which ultimately resulted in their success.

Lenore Hunter
(my first piano teacher)

I met the second teacher on my list of five when I was eight years old. She was Lenore Hunter, my first piano teacher. She and her sister, Eva, a violinist, were sort of the Pied Pipers of our neighborhood, making the rounds on our street. Traveling from house to house, their mission was to teach each one of us how to read and play music either on the violin or on the piano — a real *bargain* at just 50 cents a lesson!

In contrast to Jane Harnish, I remember Miss Hunter as being young, beautiful, and very nice. I also remember those music books which she always carried around in her brown satchel — the red ones with the shiny covers. And I remember the delight I experienced each week as *Teaching Little Fingers to Play* was indeed accomplishing its mission. I also recall the thrill of finishing that book and being promoted to the first grade book, and then on to books 2, 3, and 4.

After about two years, Miss Hunter dropped a bombshell at one of my lessons when she told my mother that she thought I was now ready to transfer to a different teacher who could work with me at a more advanced level. This indeed was a sad day because I loved Miss Hunter, the red books, and the great fun we always had together at our lessons. It seems to me that we had a near-perfect student/teacher relationship. Looking back now, I see Miss Hunter's legacy as two-fold:

1. yes, she taught me how to read and play music, but at least equally important,
2. she did this in an environment which ensured that my first piano lessons were extremely happy, positive, and productive experiences.

Again, as a teacher, although I would love for my students to remember me as young, beautiful, and very nice like Miss Hunter — still, I would much prefer being remembered as a teacher who was able to structure their lessons so that they not only experienced success, but also did so in an environment that was always positive, happy, and productive.

Helen Ringo
(my second piano teacher)

After leaving Miss Hunter, I transferred to Helen Ringo, a professor at the University of Tulsa. With her I experienced a number of firsts, including my first group lessons and even my first pedagogy class. (*By the way, one of the other students in this class was Richard Chronister. . .*) During my eight years of study with Mrs. Ringo, of course I learned much about music and playing the piano. But thinking back over this long-term relationship, I have concluded that *the environment* in which she taught me was every bit as important as what she taught me. Because she was a person who was obviously in love with music and actually with the very sound of the piano itself, this attitude permeated every lesson. It was extremely contagious and provided continuing inspiration and motivation. No wonder I remember my lessons with Helen Ringo as being the high point of every week!

The three childhood student/teacher relationships I have described so far were all essentially positive experiences and have helped to form the priorities which I hope underlie the relationships I presently have with my own students.

Isabelle Vengerova
(my third piano teacher)

After completing my study with Helen Ringo at the University of Tulsa, I became a piano student of Isabelle Vengerova in New York City. This student/teacher relationship was an entirely different kettle of fish from those three just described.

I remember my audition with "Madame" as though it was yesterday. I was asked to play practically my entire repertoire which included a Bach prelude and fugue, a Beethoven sonata (Op. 110), several Chopin etudes and the f minor Ballade, a Liszt Hungarian Rhapsody, a couple of Debussy preludes, and portions of three piano concerti (the Beethoven first, the Schumann, and the Liszt E-Flat). During the audition, Mme. said hardly a word, and then finally after two hours or so of listening to me play, she said, "I'm not at all impressed with how fast or loud you play. For this, Horowitz has already broken all of the records." (She pointed to the large photo of him in a red velvet frame which sat on her second Steinway piano.) "Besides loud and fast, what else can you do?" This question suggested to me that there was indeed life after "loud and fast" but what was it? Well, I was soon to find out when lessons began several months later.

From my first lesson with Isabelle Vengerova until I terminated my study with her three years later, I experienced both the best of times and the worst of times. The best of times were the days when I did *not* have a lesson. The worst of times were lesson days when Mme.'s persistent dissection of my playing mechanism and aural awareness became so comprehensive that I couldn't even play a scale or a two-note slur to her satisfaction. And I could go on and on, but I'm sure that by now you have gotten the picture — this was one of those *not*-so-positive student/teacher relationships.

Of some comfort during those three horrendous years was the knowledge that nearly all of her students had similar experiences. Here are some of their remembrances. In his delightful book, *I Really Should Be Practicing* (Doubleday & Co., New York, 1981), Gary Graffman writes:

> "Isabelle Vengerova...was an imposing figure. Although not very tall, she was extremely wide, and she sailed around her studio like an over-stuffed battleship in search of the enemy, cannon loaded and ready to fire...she inspired fear and trembling among even the most stouthearted. At lessons, shouts, screams, threats, curses, and stamping were the norm, and on special occasions, even the crashing of furniture could be detected."

In an article entitled "The Teaching of Isabelle Vengerova," by Joseph Rezits (*The Piano Quarterly*. Summer 1979, No. 106), another of her students, Leonard Bernstein, is quoted as saying:

> "Our first encounters were difficult. I was in mortal terror of her!"

In the same article, Rezits, another Vengerova student, solicited from 32 of her other students adjectives that they thought described her. Here are just a few of them: "a terrible taskmaster, tyrannical, an authoritarian, uncompromising, intimidating, overpowering, egotistical, sadistic, cold and cruel..." and on and on it goes.

There is no doubt that the student/teacher relationship with Isabelle Vengerova was memorable for all of her students. But for each of the negatives, I came to realize that there was also a flip side with an equal number of positives. Perhaps this additional comment from Leonard Bernstein sums it up:

> "...the Vengerova influence abides in my playing (when I play well), and I am forever in her debt."

Speaking for myself, I, too, will be forever grateful to this teacher from whom I learned so much about music and playing the piano — and about *myself* as well. Later on, this experience would inspire me to focus pedagogically on finding ways to provide my own students with many of the Vengerova *pluses,* but without so many of the negatives.

Frances Clark

The last student/teacher relationship I want to speak about is the one I had for nearly half a century with Frances Clark. I first met her in the 1940s when I was a student attending a Guy Maier workshop in Brevard, NC. In 1955, I took my first class with her which was called *Fundamentals of Piano Pedagogy*. (Incidentally, Richard Chronister was also a student in this pedagogy class!) Frances' ideas and enthusiasm about teaching not only turned me on but also were completely responsible for the changing of my career goal. My lifelong desire to become a concert pianist and to continue pursuing a concert career suddenly took a backseat to the pursuit of a career as a teacher. The obvious joy of teaching and learning which Frances exuded was inescapable. Through the years, it has become more and more clear to me that pedagogy study with Frances Clark was not just preparation for teaching — it was preparation for *life*!

In summary, student/teacher relationships always exist on a two-way street: on one side travels the teacher, and on the other, the student. From our perspective as students, the evolution of the relationships we each have had with our own most memorable teachers is an ongoing process. Surely as students, we shall continue to hear the voices of all of the significant teachers from our past as they continue to inspire, to challenge, and to teach us for as long as we continue to listen. As a teacher, to be able to achieve this with my students pretty well sums up what I would consider to be my most important priorities for my relationships with them.

CODA

I consider a masterfully taught piano lesson as being very comparable to a masterfully executed piano performance. Actually, I believe that every lesson we teach is, in reality, a performance. Over many years as a collegiate pedagogy instructor, one of my most important responsibilities was to observe piano lessons being taught by the intern teachers whom I supervised. As a result, I came to the conclusion that my evaluations of their teaching were based on pretty much the same criteria that might be used in evaluating piano performances. Below are some of the issues that were frequently addressed in the post-lesson evaluations which always followed the observation of each student's teaching.

- Was the lesson drab and dull or colorful and exhilarating?

- Was it a run-of-the-mill "ho-hum" experience or imaginative and creative?

- Was it a haphazardly thrown-together-on-the-spot event or was it obviously skillfully pre-planned, well-organized, and well-delivered?

- Was it mostly a teacher "talk-and-tell" event or a student "explore-discover-and-do" experience?

- Was it primarily *student*-centered or *teacher*-centered?

- From the student's perspective, was it a non-descript turn-off or a motivational and inspirational turn-on?

- Was the lesson an event that took place primarily in a "house of correction," or did it occur in a studio which programmed and then celebrated success and the joy of *music making*? If the latter, then it was truly an event in which both the teacher and the student came alive because of "the sound of music!"

And as a final note. . .

Perhaps one of the most important qualifications for being able to successfully teach music making at the piano is being able to do so oneself. It's usually fairly easy to "talk the talk." But do we also "walk the walk?" I am thoroughly convinced that in the last analysis, it's our own love of music and the quality of artistry and joy expressed in our performance models which both inspire and set the standards for artistic music making for our students. If this is indeed true, then it necessitates that we continue practicing what we teach for as long as we teach. Seldom will the quality of our students' performances surpass those of our own. What we are able to express with our fingers and our soul usually turns out to be far more valuable and significant than many of our words . . .

An artistic and beautiful performance is worth a thousand words!

▲ ACKNOWLEDGMENTS

The author gratefully acknowledges and thanks the following persons and events that have made the creation of this book possible:

Dorothy and Paul Truman, her parents, who could neither read nor play a note of music but who made it possible for their daughter to learn how to do both.

Diane, her fifth-grade pal and first piano student, who got this whole thing started.

All of the other students who, over the years, have taught her so much about what works and what doesn't work in the studio, but above all, about the joy of teaching!

Helen Ringo, her beloved collegiate piano teacher and first piano pedagogy instructor.

The sponsors of all of those many workshops and conferences which made us aware that we all had basically the same concerns and goals for our teaching and provided us with opportunities to come together to share our ideas and learn from each other.

Craig Sale, a long-time friend and highly respected colleague as well as a superb musician, teacher, and pianist, who served as Editor of *The Success Factor in Piano Teaching. (Craig – immense gratitude to you for both your expertise and patience in helping to get it all together.)*

Helen Marlais, another special friend and colleague who encouraged me to undertake the project of creating a book about piano teaching. *(And now, five years later, here it is, Helen!)*

Frances Clark and *Louise Goss,* two dear friends and mentors for more than half a century, whose masterful teaching and outstanding materials have served as an ongoing model of pedagogical excellence and an endless source of inspiration and professionalism in piano pedagogy.

And last but by no means least . . .
Sam Holland and *The Frances Clark Center for Keyboard Pedagogy* whose belief in the value and relevance of the "message" of *The Success Factor in Piano Teaching* for 21st century pianists and teachers has resulted in its publication. *(For the Center's sponsorship of this project, I am both humbled and grateful.)*

ABOUT THE AUTHOR

ELVINA TRUMAN PEARCE

As a Pianist . . .

Elvina Pearce grew up in Tulsa, OK, where she attended the University of Tulsa as a piano performance major. While still in her teens, she was a finalist in two major national competitions – the *Patrick Hayes Award Competition* in Washington, D.C., and the *Michaels Memorial Award Competition* in Chicago.

Upon completing her studies at the University of Tulsa, she went to New York City to become a piano student of Isabelle Vengerova, the renowned Russian artist teacher (whose students include Samuel Barber, Leonard Bernstein, Lukas Foss, and Gary Graffman).

Her concert career is highlighted by a performance of the Liszt *Piano Concerto in E-flat* with the Chicago Symphony, an "encore" performance of the Liszt in a coast-to-coast radio broadcast over WGN's "Chicago Theater of the Air," and by solo recitals in Carnegie Recital Hall in NYC, and The National Gallery of Art in Washington, D.C.

As a Teacher . . .

Following her New York study, Elvina was appointed to the piano faculty of Westminster Choir College in Princeton, NJ. While in Princeton, she studied piano pedagogy with Frances Clark, internationally acclaimed author and teacher of teachers. She subsequently became one of the founding faculty members of Dr. Clark's *New School for Music Study* in Princeton. In 1999, she helped to found the *Frances Clark Center for Keyboard Pedagogy*, serving for six years as Vice President on its Board of Trustees.

Upon moving to Illinois in the 1960s, Elvina taught at North Central College in Naperville for whom she designed and directed the college's Division of Preparatory and Community Music. For 14 years, she also taught piano and piano pedagogy at Northwestern University where she served as head of the Piano Preparatory Division.

In 2008, she was named as an *MTNA Foundation Fellow*, and in 2011, received a Lifetime Achievement Award presented by the *National Conference on Keyboard Pedagogy*. In 2014, she was inducted into the Illinois *Fox Valley Arts Hall of Fame*.

As a Clinician . . .

For more than half a century, Elvina has been active as a clinician, presenting workshops, master classes, and recitals for teachers and students in more than 40 states and Canada. She has the distinction of being the first American invited to present a non-commercial piano workshop for teachers in the Republic of China (sponsored by *Yamaha International*).

In 1999, Elvina appeared as a keynote speaker and recitalist at the *Fourth Australian National Piano Pedagogy Conference* held at the University of Western Australia in Perth. The following year, she was invited to return to Perth to conduct a week-long teachers' workshop sponsored by the *Australian Suzuki Talent Education Association.*

Elvina's numerous professional activities throughout the U.S. include presentations at state, divisional, and national conferences sponsored by *Music Teachers National Association (MTNA)*, the *National Association of Schools of Music (NASM)*, the *National Group Piano Symposium*, the *National Federation of Music Clubs*, and the *National Conference on Keyboard Pedagogy.*

As an Author and Composer . . .

A frequent contributor to national music journals, Elvina's articles on teaching have been featured in *The American Music Teacher, Clavier, Piano Guild Notes, The Piano Quarterly, The Piano Teacher, Keyboard Companion* and *Clavier Companion* magazines. She was on the editorial staff for *Keyboard Companion* for 17 years, and served as its Editor-in-Chief from 2000 to 2006. Elvina has also received national acclaim as a composer of more than twenty published collections of piano pieces for students.

SOURCES OF MUSICAL EXAMPLES USED BY PERMISSION

Chapter 6

"Fanfare in C" by Cornelius Gurlitt. *The Music Tree Part 3* by Clark, Goss & Holland; Alfred Music Publishing, 2001.

Chapter 7

"March in C" by Daniel Türk. *The Music Tree Part 3* by Clark, Goss & Holland; Alfred Music Publishing, 2001.

"Bagatelle" by Anton Diabelli. *The Music Tree Part 3: Keyboard Literature*, edited by Clark, Goss and Holland; Alfred Music Publishing, 2001.

"Morning Prayer" by Peter Tchaikovsky. *Piano Literature of the 17th, 18th and 19th Centuries*, Book 5B; edited by Clark and Goss; Alfred Music Publishing, 1957, 2000.

"Arabesque, Op. 100, No. 2" by Johann Burgmüller. *Masterwork Classics 4* edited by Magrath; Alfred Music Publishing, 1988.

"Minuet" by Bela Bartok. *The Music Tree Part 4: Keyboard Literature*, edited by Clark, Goss and Holland; Alfred Music Publishing, 2002.

"Burleske" by L. Mozart. *The Music Tree Part 4: Keyboard Literature*, edited by Clark, Goss and Holland; Alfred Music Publishing, 2002.

"Springtime in the Alps" by Jon George. *The Music Tree Part 2A* by Clark, Goss and Holland; Alfred Music Publishing, 2000.

"Invention No. 1 in C Major, BWV 772" by JS Bach. *Festival Collection Book 6*, edited by Helen Marlais; FJH Music Co., 2007.

"Gigue" by Samuel Arnold. *The Music Tree Part 3: Keyboard Literature*, edited by Clark, Goss and Holland; Alfred Music Publishing, 2001.

"Gentle Breeze" by Elvina Pearce. *Solo Flight* by Elvina Pearce; Alfred Music Publishing, 1986.

"Falling Leaves" by David Kraehenbuehl. *The Music Tree Part 4: Students' Choice*, edited by Clark, Goss and Holland; Alfred Music Publishing, 2002.

"Prayer" by Cornelius Gurlitt. *The Music Tree Part 4: Keyboard Literature*, edited by Clark, Goss and Holland; Alfred Music Publishing, 2002.

Chapter 8

"Fantasie in D Minor, K. 397" by WA Mozart. Festival Collection Book 7, edited by Helen Marlais; FJH Music Co., 2008.

"Fantasy Dance Op. 124, No. 5" by Robert Schumann. *Festival Collection Book 6*, edited by Helen Marlais; FJH Music Co., 2007.

"Notturno Op. 54, No. 4" by Edvard Grieg. *Festival Collection Book 7*, edited by Helen Marlais; FJH Music Co., 2008.

▲ CONTRIBUTORS TO THE FIRST EDITION

Cathy Albergo
Sarah Apol
Charles Aschbrenner
Susanne Baker
Jean M. Barr
Michael Benson
Gail Berenson
Bruce Berr and Jennifer Merry
Steve Betts
Anthony Birnbaum
Marvin Blickenstaff
Beverly Blumenthal
David N. Bower
Roberta Brown
Rita A. Brown
Susan Bruckner
Jane S. Brueggemann
Theresa Camilli
Tony Caramia
Patricia Carter-Zagorski
Steven Casano and Helen Chao-Casano
Valerie Cisler
Jennifer Cohen
Barbara Collins
Carla Dean Day
Alisa R. Delliquadri
Brooke Dezio
Laureen Di Bisceglie
Brenda Dillon
Carmen Doubrava
Karin Edwards
Deven Ellis
Robin Engleman
Gwendolyn J. Epps
Sonja Epting

Sara Ernst
Elizabeth Everitt
Linda Fields
Shirley H. Fike
Anna Foshee in memory
    of Georgann Gasaway
Antoinette Franke
Kathy Gault
Ann Gipson
James Goldsworthy
Carleen Graff
Marilyn Granahan
Gary Alan Graning
Helen Grosshans
Immanuela Gruenberg
Christopher Hahn
Elmer Heerema
Marilyn Henry
Andrew Hisey
Samuel S. Holland
Verna Holley
Barbara Huebner
Judith Jain
Sonnet Johnson
Beth Jones
Grace Juang
Emily Jane Katayama
Andrea Kazmaier
Mary P. Kelly
Joann Kirchner
Karen Ann Krieger
Lynn Kroeger
Yeeseon Kwon
E.L. Lancaster and Gayle Kolwalchyk
Frances Larimer

Mark Lee
Marsha Lehe
Phyllis Alpert Leherer
Gail Lew
Cheryl Cheon-Ae Lim
Maria Lonchyna-Lisowsky
James B. Lyke
Elizabeth Mackenzie
Cecilia Manalili
Barbara English Maris
Terry McRoberts
Sue Medford
Deborah Meier
Nancy Merkel
Dr. Charlie H. Mitchell
Mary Beth Molenaar
Stephanie Myers
Kim Nagy
Jon R. Nelson
Leslie V. Owsley
Marian Parrott
Diane Beyer Perett
Pamela Pike
Susan Powell
Scott Price
Cynthia Roberts
Nuria Rojas
Steve Rosenfeld
Ruth Sawyer
Kathy Sees
Hyla Sharrock
Carmen Shaw
Rebecca Shockley
Diane Smith
Elaine B. Smith
Janice Smith
Jennifer Snow
Alisha Snyder
Nancy Spahr

Iris Statland
Arlene Steffen
Lisa Studtmann
Che-Hwa Tan
Beverly Taylor
Kathleen Theisen
Karen Thickstun
Sherry Poole Todd
Angela Triandafillou
Carolyn True
Nelita True
Gayle Tuttle
John E. van der Brook
Richard Van Dyke
Susan Van Sickle
Krista Wallace-Boaz
Barbara Wardwell
Robert Weirich
William R. Weiss
Sue Liu Wen
Dale Wheeler
Nancy Whitcar
Linda Witchie
Carolyn Worthy

The Frances Clark Center for Keyboard Pedagogy, Inc.

Kingston, New Jersey